D0176000

Time Management for System Administrators

Other resources from O'Reilly

Related titles
Essential System
Administration
RT Essentials
Linux Server Hacks™
LDAP System
Administration
Asterisk: The Future of
Telephony

Switching to VoIP
SSH, The Secure Shell:
The Definitive Guide
Essential SNMP
802.11 Wireless
Networks: The Defini-
tive Guide
Exchange Server
Cookbook™

oreilly.com
oreilly.com is more than a complete catalog of O'Reilly
books. You'll also find links to news, events, articles,
weblogs, sample chapters, and code examples.

oreillynet.com is the essential portal for developers interested in open and emerging technologies, including
new platforms, programming languages, and operating systems.

Conferences
O'Reilly brings diverse innovators together to nurture
the ideas that spark revolutionary industries. We spe-
cialize in documenting the latest tools and systems,
translating the innovator's knowledge into useful skills
for those in the trenches. Visit *conferences.oreilly.com*
for our upcoming events.

Safari Bookshelf (*safari.oreilly.com*) is the premier online reference library for programmers and IT
professionals. Conduct searches across more than
1,000 books. Subscribers can zero in on answers to
time-critical questions in a matter of seconds. Read the
books on your Bookshelf from cover to cover or simply flip to the page you need. Try it today for free.

Time Management for System Administrators

Thomas A. Limoncelli

O'REILLY®

Beijing · Cambridge · Farnham · Köln · Sebastopol · Tokyo

Time Management for System Administrators
by Thomas A. Limoncelli

Copyright © 2006 O'Reilly Media, Inc. All rights reserved.
User Friendly comics Copyright © 2005 J.D. "Illiad" Frazer.
Printed in the United States of America.

Published by O'Reilly Media, Inc., 1005 Gravenstein Highway North, Sebastopol, CA 95472.

O'Reilly books may be purchased for educational, business, or sales promotional use. Online editions are also available for most titles (*safari.oreilly.com*). For more information, contact our corporate/institutional sales department: (800) 998-9938 or *corporate@oreilly.com*.

Editors:	Mike Loukides and David Brickner
Production Editor:	Marlowe Shaeffer
Cover Designer:	Karen Montgomery
Interior Designer:	David Futato

Printing History:

November 2005:   First Edition.

Nutshell Handbook, the Nutshell Handbook logo, and the O'Reilly logo are registered trademarks of O'Reilly Media, Inc. *Time Management for System Administrators*, the image of a wolverine, and related trade dress are trademarks of O'Reilly Media, Inc.

Many of the designations used by manufacturers and sellers to distinguish their products are claimed as trademarks. Where those designations appear in this book, and O'Reilly Media, Inc. was aware of a trademark claim, the designations have been printed in caps or initial caps.

While every precaution has been taken in the preparation of this book, the publisher and author assume no responsibility for errors or omissions, or for damages resulting from the use of the information contained herein.

ISBN: 978-0-596-00783-6
[LSI]

Table of Contents

Foreword

Note to self:

Dear Self, (because what else are you going to say?)

Remember to upgrade the LDAP server. Remember to patch the security hole in zlib and every other package that links to it. (On second thought, are there packages that *don't* link to it?) Remember to plan for another 10x upgrade in storage capacity. Remember to debug the boss's Outlook problems or, at the very least, have the necessary goat entrails on hand to begin the process. Remember to redo the Oracle installation. See if there are any Wikis that would work better than the one we are using. Rewrite the user account system, and this time make sure it deals with the cases they swore would never occur in the physical world. Be sure that it is Sarbanes-Oxley compliant, ISO9000 certified, and Kosher l'Pesach. Check that your staff's projects are all humming along nicely. Read the LISA conference proceedings from the last two years to make sure you aren't missing anything useful for your infrastructure. Then, if you have time left over, start planning what you are going to do next week.

No, the fact that "plan a vacation" didn't hit the list again for the 73rd consecutive week shouldn't bother you. Nor should the incident where your spouse literally tipped over laughing after hearing you were going to write a foreword for a time management book. Or should it?

Perhaps you should just take heart in the Henry Kissinger quote, "There cannot be a crisis next week. My schedule is already full."

Well, anyway. Got to get back to work.

Yours in Service,

me

Does this sound familiar to you (well, besides the spouse part, which really did happen to me)?

Tom's first book, co-written with Christine Hogan (now Lear), has become a seminal work in the sysadmin field. *The Practice of System and Network Administration* does a superb job of telling you how to build a sane and organized infrastructure by following a number of best practices. But there's only one chapter in that tome that tells you how to keep yourself sane and organized during this process. That's where this book comes in.

But why do sysadmins need their own time management book? I know I've read my fair share of generic texts on this subject over the years. In this book, Tom does an excellent job of nailing the facets of the job that make time management particularly tricky for our profession. I just want to add on to this by describing a few parts of the typical sysadmin persona that further complicates matters.

First off, most sysadmins are tenacious problem solvers. They will attach themselves to a problem like a bulldog and not let go until the problem relents. Other tasks, such as appointments and life support (like food or sleep), become secondary as they persevere, and work on the problem either in person or in their head far beyond the usual time limits. For people who habitually say, "Just one sec, I almost have this fixed," time management can be a challenge.

A second common trait I've noticed in myself and in my colleagues is a genuine desire to help people, to support them in the use of an unfriendly or unforgiving technology, and to make things work so other people can get things done. This trait is definitely commendable, but if it gets noticed that you can and are able to help, others will ask you for it more and more. The universe gravitates toward clue, so the end result is a life I usually describe as "one big tech support call." When my grandmother was still alive, I would visit her in Florida periodically. Every time I would go, she and all of her friends would bring me their digital watches to set. And you know what? I loved it. Still, one's life doesn't always run as planned when pleas for help can come at any time. I bet Superman had time management issues as well.

Closely related to system administrators' desire to help when they can is their attraction to crisis response and saving the day. Most sysadmins can't repel down the side of a building ("hut..hut..hut..") but you know they'd do it if they could. The one-person-cavalry-to-the-rescue fetish is not a sustainable rationale for staying in the profession, but it sure does a good job of initially drawing people into the field.

The last facet of the sysadmin persona I want to address is also endearing, but it tends to exasperate the sysadmin's non-sysadmin significant other(s) and flush all attempts at time management down the toilet. By and large, sysadmins find what they do to be fun. All of this tinkering, integrating, installing, building, reinstalling, puttering, etc., is fun. So fun, in fact, that they work all day and then go home and do it some more.

I once shared a bus ride with a professional chef who told me she hated to cook on her days off. "Postmen don't like to take long walks when they come home from work" is how she put it. Most of the sysadmins I know have never heard of this idea. You'll find them (and me, as my spouse would be quick to point out) curled up at home in front of a laptop "mucking about" virtually all the time. The notion of "play" and "work" are best described as a quantum superposition blur for a sysadmin. This is great because it means we enjoy what we do, but it's horrible because we can't (or won't) stop doing it. It is hard to manage your time if it is so nebulous.

So all is lost, right? Luckily, no. Time management for sysadmins would be futile if sysadmins didn't have two things on their side:

1. Themselves
2. Tom Limoncelli

As I said before, sysadmins love to tinker, organize, integrate and optimize. I have a fond memory of watching a close sysadmin friend of mine in the checkout line of a supermarket bagging his groceries. Every item was carefully considered and then placed in a bag right in the optimal spot like one big game of Tetris. If we could only turn these skills on ourselves and use them to help with the gnarly time management difficulties we face....

Well, we can. And that's where Tom comes in. He's figured out how to do just that. Tom's been working on the problems associated with time management and staying sane in this profession for years. Ever since I met him at my first LISA conference around 10 years ago, I've had the privilege of watching him grapple with this subject in several different contexts—from splitting AT&T Bell Lab's network in half to keeping a political candidate's technical infrastructure going. In each situation, he's been able to bring his years of sysadmin experience, his keen understanding of people, and a sharp sense of humor to the problem.

Now, sit back, keep your hands in the car and the safety bar down, and enjoy, as Tom helps you bring time management and sanity to your world as well.

—David N. Blank-Edelman
September 2005 (in the sysadmin profession
for 20 years)

Preface

"Time Management for System Administrators?"

Uh-huh.

"You mean, like, how to use PDAs, vCal, calendar servers, and stuff?"

No, not at all. System administrators should be able to figure those things out without needing a book.

"So why shouldn't we just buy one of the other 10 zillion time management books out on the market?"

Because they suck. Well, they don't *suck*. They just don't speak to "us." They speak to some generic person you and I can't relate to. I'm a geek. A system administrator. A networking wonk. My home life looks a lot like my work life—you should see the killer server I've set up at home. Once I've finished tweaking it, I'm going to set up the same thing at work. Very few occupations are like that. Brain surgeons don't come home excited about trying a new technique on their cat, hoping that it works so they can try it on patients.

(Shoos cat out of the room.) "I'm not letting you near my cat anymore."

Listen, what I'm trying to say is that system administration is not a job. It's a lifestyle. We need time management books that speak to our lifestyle, in our own words, and solve our problems.

"Lifestyle?"

Lifestyle, workstyle, whatever. No other job pulls people in so many directions at once. Users interrupt us constantly with requests, preventing us from getting anything done. Computers have their own needs that pull us in many directions. Our managers want us to get long-term projects done, but they flood us with requests for quick fixes that prevent us from getting to those long-term projects!

In our field, good mentors are rare. If our boss is technical, he can mentor us on technical issues but not on time management. If our boss is nontechnical, he can't mentor us because he "lacks clue" about the demands of our job.

"And what makes you so qualified?"

Well, first of all, a long time ago I took a bunch of time management training and realized that 80 percent of what was taught didn't apply to SAs. But I retained the 20 percent that did. Then, over the years, I've refined the techniques, developed a lot of my own, and even started teaching seminars on the topic. This book captures what's in that training.

"Well, you still haven't convinced me."

Let me give you an example. You know the difference between an interpreted language and a compiled language, right?

"Sure! Interpreted languages are slower because they have to reinterpret each line of code every time they see it. Compiled languages spend a lot of time up front processing the entire program and turning it into machine language, which then can run much more quickly than the interpreted counterpart."

Exactly.

"So you want me to compile my life?"

That would be cool, but no. But we can learn a lot from compilers—spend a little time up front so you don't have to repeat a process multiple times later. For example, at a previous site, it was my job to change the backup tapes. This was before inexpensive tape jukeboxes eliminated a lot of that work. We had three main servers in the computer room, plus eight small servers scattered around the building. A tape didn't need to be changed if there was "a lot of room" left, but it took a long time and a lot of guesswork to predict if I could skip changing the tape for that server. If I misjudged how much free tape would be needed to complete tomorrow's backups, some of them would fail. Failure was bad—I didn't want that! The process really stressed me out. Then I realized that I was acting like an interpreter revisiting every step each day, stressing out over each detail. I needed to do the analysis once and stick with those decisions.

The first decision I made was "tape is cheap, my time isn't." So, rather than try to optimize every bit of tape, I was going to waste a little tape and gain a lot of time.

The next decision I made was "don't sweat the small stuff." The data in those eight small servers scattered around the complex were a lot less important than the data in the computer room. Yet, I was stressing out about them. I had to stop caring (and stressing) about the things that didn't matter. SAs have trouble setting priorities.

I decided I needed to do analysis once and reuse it every day. I needed to be like a compiled language instead of an interpreted language: precompile a decision and use it over and over. My analysis was that the servers in the computer room needed to be changed almost every day. Therefore, I would change them every day without doing any analysis of how much space was left on the tapes. If I wasted a little tape, I wasn't going to care.

However, the smaller, scattered servers rarely needed changing. I would change those tapes every Monday, plus the day after any of the backups failed due to a full tape.

"So you decided that failure was OK."

Yes. I stopped worrying about perfection where it didn't matter. Perfectionism is often overkill and a real time waster.

The inventors of the Internet were brilliant at this. They realized they'd never get anywhere if they waited for the underlying communication links to be perfect, and so they developed protocols that worked around imperfections.

"But my boss expects perfection."

Actually, your boss has priorities, too, and she realizes that tradeoffs must be made. We'll talk about managing your boss in Chapter 8.

"Please tell me that all your advice there won't relate to compilers and interpreters."

Oh, I promise. Not everything will be an analogy. However, you will see some important themes:

- Keep all your time-management stuff in one place.
- Use your brain for what you are working on right now, and use external storage for everything else.
- Develop routines for things that happen periodically.
- Pre-compute decisions by developing habits and mantras.
- Maintain focus during project time.
- Improve your social life by applying these tools outside of work, too.

"Are you going to work that into some cute acronym?"

I promise I won't. What's important to know for now is that I have constructed each chapter to group together particular problem areas for system administrators. They build on each other.

Preface

An introduction to the book and the topics covered in it. You're reading this right now.

Chapter 1, *Time Management Principles*

What makes us so special? It's mostly the volume of interruptions we get and the huge number of simultaneous projects we're asked to do. But there's more to it than that. This chapter introduces the principles that will be used throughout the rest of the book.

Chapter 2, *Focus Versus Interruptions*

This chapter teaches you how to deal with an interrupting customer without sounding like a jerk. You won't be able to accomplish much without managing your interruptions.

Chapter 3, *Routines*

This chapter shows you how to turn chaos into routine. Our jobs are full of chaos—anything we can turn into a routine means a little less chaos and a lot less stress. When we develop routines for our tasks, they become habits and we're less likely to forget them.

Chapter 4, *The Cycle System*

This chapter introduces you to my "Cycle System," which is a way to manage your to do list. It teaches you how to juggle many demands without dropping anything. Even if you have 100 hours of tasks on your plate, you can manage them all and still work only 8 hours a day.

Chapter 5, *The Cycle System: To Do Lists and Schedules*

This chapter focuses upon the actual day-to-day work of putting The Cycle System into practice, creating your schedule and to do list. It also gives you tips and strategies for dealing with too much work.

Chapter 6, *The Cycle System: Calendar Management*

SAs have lots of meetings and appointments. If we can manage them better, not only do we no longer miss appointments, but we can schedule more fun into our social lives. In this chapter, I extend The Cycle System to include our calendar.

Chapter 7, *The Cycle System: Life Goals*

This chapter teaches you how to identify long-term goals, both personal and professional, and how to make sure you achieve them. Where do you want to be in 10 years? You're more likely to get there if you do a little bit of planning now.

Chapter 8, *Prioritization*

> A good juggler can juggle many objects but has to stop the whole juggle when a single mistake is made. A great juggler knows how to extend a juggle by dropping a ball or two so the others can stay in play. In this chapter, I discuss a few different ways to prioritize so that The Cycle System works even better.

Chapter 9, *Stress Management*

> A short chapter about how I learned to manage stress.

Chapter 10, *Email Management*

> We all get too much email. Here are a few realistic tips for getting control over the flood of email you receive.

Chapter 11, *Eliminating Time Wasters*

> One way to have more time is to eliminate time wasters. In this chapter, I talk about how to identify and eliminate them.

Chapter 12, *Documentation*

> This chapter explores ways to document without pain. When we document, we help our time management two ways. First, we spend less time trying to remember how to do something because we can refer to our notes. Second, it makes it easier to have someone else take over the task, completely removing it from our to do list. The problem is finding a realistic way to get in the habit of documenting. The solution is called a Wiki.

Chapter 13, *Automation*

> What's better than having a computer do your job for you? There are many novel and easy ways to start automating tasks today, even if you don't know a lot about programming. This chapter explains a few methods to automate a lot with little effort.

Epilogue

> A few concluding suggestions about what to do with the free time you'll have after applying the techniques in this book.

How to Read This Book

"Is all this really going to help me?"

Absolutely! Amazingly enough, if you read this book, your entire life will be transformed instantly and all of your problems will be fixed. You'll be better looking, too!

"Really?"

No. This book won't fix all your problems instantly. In fact, I hope you've dealt with enough salespeople to know that anyone who promises that a product works instantly and solves all of your problems isn't telling the truth.

"So what *will* this book do?"

This book will give you a framework for managing your time. It's a system that works for me and others, and it can be adopted to your workstyle. The techniques will replace your old, bad habits with better habits. The truth is that you've spent your entire life developing the bad habits that are with you today, and it will take some time to develop good ones. In fact, psychologists tell us that it takes 21 days of doing a new behavior to develop it into a habit.

"So, I'm 21 days away from...."

Well, for you, it may take longer. Did I ever tell you the story of my first experience with time management?

"No."

I took a two-day class. For a month afterward, I didn't use a single technique. It just seemed like too much work to change my ways! Then I had a really busy week, with more things to do than I could keep track of. So, I pulled out the leather-bound organizer that I received as part of the class and struggled to remember some of the techniques. Using the workbook from the class, I pieced together what I was supposed to have learned.

"And what happened?"

I got more done in that day than I had in ages, and I was much less stressed about the tasks I put off for later.

Over the next few months, I kept going back to the course book to refresh my memory or pick up new techniques. It was a struggle but eventually the techniques became second nature. More importantly, I found new techniques that are specific to system administration. Soon I was teaching my techniques to coworkers, then I found myself teaching seminars—now it's all here in this book.

"How long before you didn't have to think so hard to do the techniques?"

About a month. About a year. It depended on which technique. I expect that's how people will use this book. You'll read it—ignore half of it—then keep coming back to it for "new" advice. It took me a few decades to develop my bad habits. It took quite some time to break those habits and develop new ones.

The sooner you get started, the sooner the change will come. Start today.

"Well, that all sounds really good, but with people stopping by my office every five minutes, I'm not going to have time to read this book."

That's a good point. Let's make a deal: I'll cover dealing with interruptions in the first chapter, and you promise to try every technique at least once.

"It's a deal."

Audience

This book is for IT workers, system administrators, network administrators, operators, help desk personnel, and the many, many other similar job titles that can be found in the IT industry. It is written for people who are early in their career, but industry veterans will find these techniques to be equally useful. If you don't think you have time to read this book, you need this book.

This book is not for programmers. Beta readers told me that programmers should find this book extremely useful, but I feel that programmers have different issues and therefore deserve their own book. If you're a programmer, buy this book as a gift for the system administrator who supports you. If you happen to read it before it gets gift-wrapped, I won't tell.

About This Book

This is a "technique" book. The art of time management can be done with a paper and pencil or a fancy PDA. The first part of the book helps you deal with the basics of time management—better ways to deal with the interruptions that keep you from getting work done, and managing your to do list so that you don't forget any requests and are able to get them done on time, or at least based on your priorities. This book will help you turn chaotic, unplanned activities into easier-to-use routines that are less likely to be forgotten. After that, I expand the techniques and teach you to apply them to managing your calendar/datebook, email, stress, and life goals. Lastly, I cover techniques that can accelerate your career: eliminating time wasters, using documentation to save yourself time, and tips for automating what you do so that it is less error prone and takes less of your time.

Now that you know what this book is about, I should explain what this book is not about. This book is not about how to use a PDA, nor which personal information management software to use. It is not a comparison of 50 to do list management software packages. It is not "the missing manual" for PalmOS or Microsoft Windows Mobile 2003 Second Edition Operating System. This book is about you and how to improve your life through better time management.

Assumptions This Book Makes

This book makes no assumptions about the expertise and/or technical savvy of the reader. However, people earlier in their system administration career may find it more useful. The more stressed out you are about your job, the more valuable this book will be.

Chapter 13 contains actual code samples, so some prior knowledge is required to understand and apply these examples, but they're nothing the typical administrator doesn't already know.

Conventions Used in This Book

The following typographical conventions are used in this book:

Plain text
> Indicates menu titles, menu options, menu buttons, and keyboard accelerators (such as Alt and Ctrl).

Italic

> Indicates new terms, URLs, email addresses, filenames, file extensions, pathnames, directories, and Unix utilities.

`Constant width`

> Indicates commands, options, switches, variables, attributes, keys, functions, types, classes, namespaces, methods, modules, properties, parameters, values, objects, events, event handlers, XML tags, HTML tags, macros, the contents of files, or the output from commands.

`Constant width bold`

> Shows commands or other text that should be typed literally by the user.

`Constant width italic`

> Shows text that should be replaced with user-supplied values.

 This icon signifies a tip, suggestion, or general note.

 This icon indicates a warning or caution.

Using Code Examples

This book is here to help you get your job done. In general, you may use the code in this book in your programs and documentation. You do not need to contact us for permission unless you're reproducing a significant portion of the code. For example, writing a program that uses several chunks of code from this book does not require permission. Selling or distributing a CD-ROM of examples from O'Reilly books *does* require permission. Answering a question by citing this book and quoting example code does not require permission. Incorporating a significant amount of example code from this book into your product's documentation *does* require permission.

We appreciate, but do not require, attribution. An attribution usually includes the title, author, publisher, and ISBN. For example: *"Time Management for System Administrators* by Thomas A. Limoncelli. Copyright 2006 O'Reilly Media, Inc., 0-596-00783-3."

If you feel your use of code examples falls outside fair use or the permission given above, feel free to contact us at *permissions@oreilly.com.*

We'd Like to Hear from You

Please address comments and questions concerning this book to the publisher:

O'Reilly Media, Inc.
1005 Gravenstein Highway North
Sebastopol, CA 95472
(800) 998-9938 (in the U.S. or Canada)
(707) 829-0515 (international or local)
(707) 829-0104 (fax)

We have a web page for this book, where we list errata, examples, and any additional information. You can access this page at:

http://www.oreilly.com/catalog/timemgmt

To comment or ask technical questions about this book, send email to:

bookquestions@oreilly.com

You can contact the author at his web site or via email:

Web: *http://www.everythingsysadmin.com*
Email: *timebook@everythingsysadmin.com*

For more information about our books, conferences, Resource Centers, and the O'Reilly Network, see our web site at:

http://www.oreilly.com

Safari® Enabled

 When you see a Safari® Enabled icon on the cover of your favorite technology book, that means the book is available online through the O'Reilly Network Safari Bookshelf.

Safari offers a solution that's better than e-books. It's a virtual library that lets you easily search thousands of top tech books, cut and paste code samples, download chapters, and find quick answers when you need the most accurate, current information. Try it for free at *http://safari.oreilly.com*.

Acknowledgments

This book would not be possible without the help of Chris Polk, who supported me both emotionally and technically throughout the entire project. Every chapter was influenced by her helpful suggestions.

Thanks to David Blank-Edelman for his touching Foreword, and to Illiad for his *User Friendly* comic strips. I feel doubly blessed to have both of you involved.

I'd also like to thank the O'Reilly staff for their help, especially Mike Loukides for bringing this project to O'Reilly and helping to define the book, and David Brickner who got the book into shape so it could be published. David took an OK book and turned it into a great book. I couldn't have done it without him. Marlowe Shaeffer, my production editor, brought these pages to life. Thanks to everyone at O'Reilly!

If I see farther than others, it's because I stand on the shoulders of greatness. Some of these great people are: Mary Clark, Benji Feen, Doug Furlong, Trey Harris, Jennifer Joy, Andy Lester, R. A. Lichtensteiger, John Linderman, Les Lloyd, Ralph Loura, David Malone, Tina Mancuso, Cliff Miller, Adam Moskowitz, Daisy Nguyen, Cat Okita, JP, Victor Raymond, Tom Reingold, Michael Richichi, Strata Rose-Chalup, Glenn Seib, Frank J. T. Wojcik, and apologies to anyone I have forgotten!

## CHAPTER 1

Time Management Principles

Wait! Before we get started, let's do something to make sure we actually finish.

I realize that as a system administrator (SA), you are flooded with constant interruptions. The phone rings, a customer* stops by with questions, your email reader beeps with the arrival of a new message, and someone on Instant Messenger (IM) is trying to raise your attention. Heck, I bet someone's interrupted you while reading this paragraph.

I'm not going to cover how to deal with interruptions until the next chapter, and I hope you don't take offense, but at this rate, I'm worried you won't get that far. To mitigate this problem I'm going to share a tip from Chapter 2, which, if you implement, will shield you from interruptions between now and when we can deal with the subject of interruptions properly.

Suppose you are in an environment with two SAs. You and your coworker can agree to establish a *mutual interruption shield*. Before lunch, you field all the interruptions so that your coworker can work on projects. After lunch, your coworker fields all the interruptions and lets you work on projects. Obviously, if there is an emergency or an urgent request that only you can handle, you'll drop what you're doing. However, you'll find that by organizing your days like this, you'll see an immediate improvement in the amount of project work you get done. You may also find some time to read this book.

This method works particularly well when there are a lot of SAs. I was once part of a very large admin team, and we were able to assign time slots of

---

* In this book, I will use the term "customer" to denote any internal or external user of your computers, network, applications, and so on. I prefer "customer" over "user" because it better represents the relationship SAs should have with the people they serve.

"interruption catching" that let the entire rest of the team focus on project work for all but one hour a day.

This method can be adapted to a solo SA, too. If you are a solo SA, talk with your manager about how you could improvise some kind of equivalent system. For example, management can make the users aware that afternoons are reserved for "project time," and non-urgent requests should be emailed to you (or to your request-tracking system) for processing the next morning. This might match the natural flow of an office. For example, if most interruptions happen in the morning, it will be easier to schedule the afternoon as "project time." It may be more appropriate to do that only when a special, visible project is coming due. For example, your boss assigns you a project that will benefit many aspects of the company. This is an opportunity to ask for special dispensation so that the project can get done quickly.

There are also physical things you can do to protect your "project time." Obviously, if you have an office, you can close your door to prevent casual drop-ins and social visits. A more effective technique is to make sure that customers must walk past your Tier 1 (customer-facing) system administrators in order to get to Tier 2 people (you). If you are the senior SA, re-arrange your seating so that people must pass by a junior SA on their way to you. The role of a junior SA is to handle 80 percent of the interruptions and let the 20 percent that only you can do, get to you. Physical location is key to this. Walk 50 feet from your desk, turn around, and walk back to where you sit while imagining you are a typical customer. What do you see? Make sure it is the person who is supposed to be customer-facing and working on all the Tier 1 support requests.

Go away and arrange your mutual interruption shield right now. I'll wait.

Hey, what part of "right now" didn't you understand? You didn't make that arrangement, did you? Please do it now before you continue. I really want you to be able to read this book.

USER FRIENDLY by Illiad

What's So Difficult About Time Management?

Ah, now we can really begin!

Time management is difficult for SAs because we are constantly being interrupted. How can we get anything done if we are constantly pausing to fix emergencies or respond to requests that arrive in person, via email, or via the newest source of interruptions, instant messages (IMs)? How many times have you told your boss that a project would take two uninterrupted days to complete, which means a month of actual time? Returning to a task takes a long time. If an interruption takes one minute, and it takes two minutes to return to your project, you're actually traveling backward in time! H. G. Wells would be impressed! Worst of all, returning to your project after an interruption can lead to errors. Often, when I'm debugging a problem, I find the actual "error" was that I skipped a step after returning from an interruption!

Management judges an SA by whether projects get done. Customers, however, judge you by whether you are available to them. These two priorities play against each other, and you're stuck in the middle. If you are infinitely available to customers, you will never have time to complete the projects that management wants to see completed. Yet, who approves your pay raises?

Why a book on time management just for SAs? This book needs to be different from your average "time management" book because SAs are different. In particular:

- **Our problems are different.** SAs have an unusually high number of interruptions that prevent us from getting our projects done.

- **Our solutions are different.** SAs can handle more high-tech solutions such as request trackers, email filtering with procmail, automation scripts, and other tools unsuitable for the average, non-technical person.

- **We lack quality mentoring.** SAs need to learn the fundamentals of to do list management, calendar management, and life-goal management just like anyone else. However, our normal career path usually doesn't lend itself to learn these things. Our mentors are technical peers, often on email lists, and often in different parts of the world. There are fewer opportunities to learn by watching, as a supervisor often learns from a director.

The Principles of Time Management for SAs

There are six principles that I base all my techniques on. I don't claim that any of these are my own invention, but I certainly put my own spin on them. You will see these principles throughout the book:

- One "database" for time management information (use one organizer).
- Conserve your brain power for what's important (conserve RAM).
- Develop routines and stick with them (reuse code libraries; don't reinvent the wheel).
- Develop habits and mantras (replace runtime calculations with precomputed decisions).
- Maintain focus during "project time" (be like a kernel semaphore).
- Manage your social life with the same tools you use for your work life (social life isn't an optional feature).

Let's take a look at each one of these principles in greater detail.

One "Database" for Time Management Information

The central tool for time management is your Personal Digital Assistant (PDA) or Personal Analog Assistant (PAA), which you will use to store your to do list, calendar, and life goals lists. I'm sure you know what a PDA is: a Palm Pilot, Zaurus, or similar product. A PAA is the paper equivalent. You've seen these in many shapes and forms and by names such as organizer, binder, planner, datebook, or even Filofax.

Whether you choose to use a PDA or PAA, it will become the platform for just about every technique in the rest of the book. By putting all your information in one place, you won't have to jump between different systems. If you have disorganized habits, this will be the tool for getting organized. If you are overly organized, this will be your tool for slimming down to a simple, basic system that saves you time and prevents you from spending time organizing your organization.

I'm going to use the term *organizer* to mean either a PDA or PAA. It doesn't matter how hi-tech or low-tech you go. When I specifically mention PDA or PAA, I'll be referring to a technique or example that can only be performed with that particular kind of organizer.

We're going to make sure that your organizer is something you can trust. What you write in your organizer won't be forgotten, deleted, or lost, and it won't disappear like invisible ink. Until you trust your organizer, you aren't going to be as facile with the rest of your time management techniques. Developing this trust, like forming a new habit, takes time.

Conserve Your Brain Power for What's Important

It's important to have an uncluttered brain. A cluttered brain is full of distractions that prevent you from staying focused. You're going to learn to use external storage for anything you aren't focused on right now.

Don't take it personally, but your brain isn't as good at recalling things as a piece of paper or a computer. Don't use your brain to track tasks or appointments. Use your organizer, a request-tracking database, a Wiki, or anything other than your brain.

Your brain only has a certain amount of capacity. It's either RAM or CPU power, depending on how you envision the brain. If you clutter your brain with the knowledge of all the tasks you need to do in the future, that's taking space away from the task you are working on right now.

In fact, when I'm working on Project A but worried about Project B, the best thing I can do is to write Project B down in my to do list and try to get it out of my head. Then, I can focus on Project A. I trust the to do list to "remember" B for me, so I don't have to continue to waste mental energy on it.

It might be apocryphal, but it is believed that Albert Einstein's closet contained seven identical suits—one for each day of the week. This was, the story goes, so that he could conserve his brain power for physics and not waste it on the mundane task of deciding what to wear each day. Maybe this is why Steve Jobs always wears black turtlenecks. (Personally, I have many pairs of the exact same socks, but that's just so I never have more than one unmatched sock when I do laundry.)

With the help of this book, you're going to eliminate the excuse "I forgot" from your vocabulary. You may miss a deadline for other reasons, but it won't be because you were trying to remember so many things that it slipped your mind.

Getting tasks, instructions, and knowledge out of your brain and onto paper or in a digital repository is the first step to getting help with those tasks. While our brains are single-user, and no one, I hope, can read our minds, external formats are multiuser and open up the possibility of others helping us with our work. For example, documenting a procedure and putting it on a web site means other people can study and hopefully do the procedure. Using a request-tracker database means other SAs can take items, customers can see the progress of their requests, and management can gather statistics. Why try to memorize the list of services that need to be tested after an operating system is upgraded? Keep the list in a spreadsheet rather than your brain. Now you can share the spreadsheet with others to see if you are missing anything.

Develop Routines and Stick with Them

A good software developer tries to be lazy: if a bit of code works, he reuses it as often as possible. I write a lot of Perl code. People think I'm a Perl expert. The reality is that I know about 10 really good Perl idioms, and I reuse them over and over. Rarely is a program truly written from scratch. You're going to manage your time the same way. You're going to turn regular activity into routines so you spend less time planning things that are going to happen anyway.

I used to spend hours each week playing phone tag to figure out when I could talk with my boss. Now we meet at the same time every week for a brief status meeting. No more guessing. It's a routine we have. Establishing this routine saves us both time and reduces the "thinking" we have to do each week.

To make sure that I don't spend a lot of time managing all my time management techniques, I work them into a routine, too. At the start of the day, before I've even checked my email, I review my to do list and set priorities for the day.

It's important to stick with your routines because other people start to count on them. That helps them plan their days. Everyone is helped.

Develop Habits and Mantras

Habits are routines you do without having to think. Mantras are mental triggers for rules of thumb.

I refill my gas tank every Sunday. It's a good habit. Sometimes I can't even remember why I do it, but I trust the habit and use it. Ah! That's right! It all started because I was often late for work on Monday morning and didn't want to be *more* late because I had to stop to fill my tank. Now it's a habit. Unless my tank is completely full, I always fill my tank on Sunday.

Rules of thumb are like habits that don't happen regularly. They are ways to mentally record responses that are generally good for particular situations. When I activate a rule of thumb, I have a mantra, or saying, that goes along with it. For small tasks that I'm likely to procrastinate on, my mantra is:

Sooner is better than later.

For example, I once had to periodically empty the water-collection bucket on a portable air-conditioning unit in a small computer closet. (Yes, in the long term, the better solution is to install a drain pipe or to use a cooler that evaporates the water into the exhaust. This was a temporary solution.) The bucket had two levels—"Time to empty the bucket," and "You idiot, you should have emptied it already." It could take a week before the water level reached the first mark, which gave me a good excuse to ignore the bucket for days at a time. This caused three problems. First, emptying the bucket when it was very full was much more difficult than emptying it when it was fairly full—splish-splash. Second, as luck would have it, most times I noticed that the water level was too high to ignore, it always seemed to be at the end of the day when I had to be somewhere after work. Now I would be late because I had to spend 15 minutes emptying the water. Third and most important, I ran the constant risk of overflowing the bucket. Though a detector on the unit automatically shut off the air-conditioning before the bucket overflowed, this fail-safe could result in a room temperature hot enough to fry all the computers.

As you can guess, all of this was improved when I employed my "Sooner is better than later" mantra. The first time I noticed the water level above the first mark, I said to myself, "Sooner is better than later" and emptied the bucket. Problem solved. This mantra is closely related to the adage, "A stitch in time saves nine."

Eventually habits and mantras become second nature. Developing habits and mantras are investments we make so that our brain isn't cluttered in the long run. When they become second nature, they stay out of the way of our usual thoughts and thus don't risk violating our principle to conserve RAM.

Here's another mantra that has served me well:

Trust the process.

In a few chapters, I'll recommend spending five minutes each morning planning your day. Ironically, it is the hectic days when you are most tempted to skip the five minutes of planning, yet it is those days that planning is most beneficial. I say to myself, "Trust the process," and do the planning. I'm always glad I did.

When your brain is full of negative or toxic thoughts such as, "I'll do it later," or "I'm too busy to stop for five minutes to plan my day," a mantra has the power to fill your brain with a positive thought, squeezing out the negativity. If you can act during the fleeting moment that the mantra fills your brain, you'll be taking positive action before the negative thought can return.

That's a really important point. You can train yourself to fake out your brain!

Maintain Focus During "Project Time"

Earlier in this chapter I talked about the importance of managing interruptions. That's all part of maintaining focus. Interruptions are the natural enemy of focus. You'll learn to use your organizer and other techniques to maintain focus.

Distractions are so, um, distracting! Think about how an operating system works. When time-critical operations need to be done, the kernel locks out all other tasks and works on exactly one task until that task is complete. For example, when memory is being allocated to a task, the kernel locks out all other memory-table access so that this one happens correctly, without multiple processes all trying to modify the allocation tables at the same time. As an SA, you want the same kind of laser focus when you're working.

Operating system designers go to great lengths to make sure that a process can return from an interruption quickly (especially the constant swapping between processes in a multitasking operating system). They do this because they know that time spent returning from an interruption is wasted time and should be minimized. You should do the same.

Manage Your Social Life with the Same Tools You Use for Your Work Life

Last but not least, don't forget to have fun. The same tools we use to make sure there's enough time for our important projects at work can be used to make sure we don't miss out on the social life and family life that we want to have.

No one's dying thought is, "Gosh, I wish I had spent more time at the office."

By using the same tools for organizing your work and non-work life, you increase the practice you get at using these techniques! The more practice, the faster you develop better organization habits. You are also leveraging some good, proven techniques rather than reinventing the wheel.

This isn't to say that your social life will become structured and scheduled down to the minute. There's nothing wrong with scheduling an evening of goofing off!

It Won't Be Easy

I'm told that when teaching, it's better to tell people how difficult it's going to be early in the process so that they aren't so disappointed when they realize it isn't all milk and honey (or Jolt and chocolate). I'm told that it's a lot better than promising people "easy, fast results" and having them give up at the first challenge, possibly blaming themselves for not achieving the instant results promised.

Therefore, let me be perfectly clear: this may be the most difficult journey on which you've ever embarked. You've spent your entire life developing the bad time management habits you have right now; you can't fight that inertia over night. It's going to take long hours of practice. You are going to stumble through a lot of this, come back a month later, reread a chapter, and realize that you've been doing it wrong. At times it will seem like there is no hope, that these techniques are a waste of time and more difficult than just muddling though the old way.

I can assure you that you'll have all these feelings because I felt them all, too.

But now I'm writing this book. I must have survived. So will you.

Every time things look grim and difficult, just remember that change comes in small steps. Keep trying. Stick with the program. Squeeze those negative thoughts from your brain by saying to yourself, "Trust the process" and give it another try.

When you least expect it, someone will say to you, "You're so organized! I wish I knew how you do it all so well!" and you'll realize that you haven't had to refer back to this book in ages. Success!

Summary

- Time management is particularly difficult for system administrators because we have unique problems (a mix of projects and interruptions), our technical mentors don't have good time management skills, and our nontechnical managers don't understand our work. One asset at our disposal is that we are highly technical people and can easily use technical solutions to manage our time.

- External interruptions (customers) and self-imposed interruptions (Instant Messages, new email notifications, and so on) kill productivity. Returning from an interruption takes time and introduces errors into your work.

Poker Chips

Everyone has advice about how to avoid procrastination. Search Google for "avoiding procrastination" and you'll get back over 19,000 links. You'll find work sheets from university counseling centers that help you get in touch with the sources of your procrastination. You'll find books and articles. You'll find top 10 lists of reasons why people procrastinate and how to counteract them. You'll find professional life coaches who will (in person or via phone) coach you through this and other life difficulties (for a fee). Feel free to try what appeals to you. In fact, do that right now.

I think the most important thing to remember is that procrastination is natural. It comes from fear and self-doubt. We all fear change. We all doubt our ability to succeed.

Instead of focusing on your self-doubt, focus on its opposite—your *self-esteem*. Self-esteem is like a stack of poker chips. If you are playing poker and you only have a few chips, you can only make small bets. This means you can't win a lot of money. In fact, you'll have to fold more often rather than risk losing your last chip. When you have a lot of chips, you can make big bets that pay off big. You can take risks. You can try things that you wouldn't have tried when you had fewer chips. You can win big!

When we have little self-esteem, we are more likely to give up or not even try. Without trying, we are never in the position to succeed. So, we don't. When we have high self-esteem, we're more willing to take risks and put ourselves in a position to have the opportunity to win.

Understand why self-esteem is like a big pile of poker chips?

Here's the magic: the poker chips of self-esteem only exist in your head, so you can create more!

In poker, the chips are real, physical objects. You can't just twinkle your nose and make poker chips appear. On the other hand, in life, you can do any kind of ritual to make more self-esteem chips appear magically. My "Sooner is better than later" mantra gives me the chips I need to overcome procrastination. A hug from someone you love magically makes more chips appear. The quiet support of a friend helping you to sit down and read this book makes even more chips appear. Therapy is all about increasing your chips. If shouting out loud, "Yes, I can!" makes more self-esteem chips, then shout all you want.

Pretty neat, eh?

Experts agree: buying this book automagically gives you a huge boost to the number of poker chips you have at your disposal. Turn the page and get to work.

- Arrange a mutual interruption shield with coworkers so that someone else deflects interruptions when you need to get projects done.
- Use one database for all time management information. Keeping everything in one place helps you stay organized.
- Conserve brain power for what's important. Use your brain for the work on hand and an organizer to record to do items, dates, and notes.
- Develop routines and stick with them. Rather than constantly reinventing the wheel or repeating decision-making processes, work things into routines.
- Develop habits and mantras. They help remind you to reuse previous good decisions.
- Maintain focus during "project time." You will work better when you focus on one thing at a time.
- Manage your social life with the same tools you use for your work life. Your non-work life is important, and you should manage it with the same tools you use for your work life so that you don't miss out on the fun things either.

CHAPTER 2

Focus Versus Interruptions

How many times have you told your boss that something will take a day of uninterrupted time, which means it will be done a month from now? SAs say this because their project work is constantly interrupted with requests from customers and management alike.

But when a system administrator says, "Users are always bothering me!" what he really means is, "I wish I could maintain focus on my tasks."

When we are focused and can work uninterrupted, we can get anything done. Focus is concentrated effort. When we are focused, we get our work done in less time, and our newly found free time can be used for more work or social activities. It's like eliminating unused peripherals from your laptop—the battery lasts longer and you can do more work or spend more time playing a game.

Interruptions are the natural enemy of focus. They steal time from us both directly and indirectly. The direct way they steal time is obvious: an interruption that stalls us for t minutes delays task completion by t minutes. That's easy. However, the indirect way that they steal time is more insidious. When you return from an interruption, you have to spend p minutes to figure out where you left off. If you were interrupted during the third step of a multipart process, do you return to step three or step four? Figuring out where you left off is extra work that steals time from the project. I confess that in my career as an SA the biggest technical mistakes I've made can be traced to an interruption that led me to skip a step or forget to verify the previous step I had been working on. I returned to step four instead of three—oops. If the time spent recovering from those mistakes is s, then the total delay as the result of an interruption is $t+p+s$, which can be longer than the task itself!

Unfortunately, as an SA, interruptions are a fact of life. We must deal with our customers' needs—it's a job requirement. But balancing those needs with our project goals can be a hassle and a strain on personal relations with our coworkers. You might say that this chapter teaches you how to keep yourself focused and deal with interruptions without being a jerk.

USER FRIENDLY by Illiad

SO GREG, ACCORDING TO YOUR LIST, YOU'RE WORKING ON PRUNING THE TROUBLE TICKET DATABASE. HOW LONG WILL YOU NEED?

FOUR WEEKS.

OKAY, LET ME REPHRASE. HOW LONG WILL YOU NEED ONCE WE REMOVE QUAKE III ARENA FROM YOUR MACHINE?

A COUPLE HOU--I MEAN, FOUR WEEKS!

COPYRIGHT © 2002 ILLIAD HTTP://WWW.USERFRIENDLY.ORG/

The Focused Brain

Focus is about dedicating as much of your brain as possible to a particular task. The brain has many parts: the front part is dealing with whatever you are thinking about right now (the CPU and L1/L2 cache, if you will), the back part is where you store stuff (the RAM), and the far back part is where you store long-term knowledge (your hard drive). Focus deals with what I'll unscientifically call the front of your brain.

When you focus, you are trying to dedicate 100 percent of the front of your brain to your current task. To best understand this, let's look at an unfocused brain. Pretend you're trying to concentrate on a task, for example, writing a new Perl program to automate a procedure. However your mind is also cluttered with thoughts about the meeting you have in an hour, the three other tasks you have to do today, the milk you must buy on the way home, and you are still worrying about something your boss said to you this morning. All those things are taking up space in the front part of your brain, stealing capacity away from that Perl program you are writing! How good do you think that Perl program is going to be with all that other stuff filling up the front of your brain?

You wouldn't think that just trying to remember that you need to buy milk after work would take cycles away from your task at hand, but it does. Part of the brain is used to keep that memory alive. DRAM chips work the same way. They have to keep refreshing their memory or the information disappears. (Interestingly enough, SRAM doesn't require constant refreshing and is much more expensive.) Keeping a memory alive in the front of your brain is just as much "work" as doing any other physical task.

Clear all those "need to remember" things out of your brain by delegating responsibility for remembering to some other system. Set an alarm to ring before the meeting starts, write those three tasks on a to do list (see Chapter 5), write "milk" on your shopping list, and write down that you are going to visit your boss first thing in the morning to find out what he really meant (see Chapter 8). Now, you can rid your mind of those items and free up space for that task you're working on. Don't worry about forgetting those things; trust the systems you've delegated them to.

Sure, you're a smart person. You *might* be able to remember all those things and work at the same time, but why would you want to? I'm dumb as toast compared to most people I work with, but I use these techniques to level the playing field. If you are a smart person, you can have the effectiveness of people who are super-smart. And if you are super-smart, well, why are you reading this book? Give the rest of us a break!

Difficulty Falling Asleep?

Falling asleep is about letting your brain calm down. How can you calm down if you are expecting it to remember something for tomorrow? You can't do both at once.

Keep a pad of paper and a pen next to your bed. When something is keeping you awake, write it down and try falling asleep again. I bet you'll be asleep soon.

This technique also works if something is worrying you or making you angry. Worry keeps us awake because we're trying to remember to do something about what's worrying us. Anger keeps us awake because we're trying to remember to stay angry! If you write down what's worrying you or making you angry, your brain can relax a little because you know the pad of paper will be there in the morning.

Even better—call your phone number at work and leave yourself voice mail. This works from anywhere there is a phone. This also eliminates the chance that you'll forget to take your note into work!

Many cell phones and MP3 players include voice recorders. Get in the habit of using them so you don't lose your good ideas.

An Environment to Encourage Focus

Lack of focus doesn't just come from external interruptions. We are also to blame—we turn on music, we have magically updating screen backgrounds, we have IRC chat rooms scrolling and instant message clients trying to catch our attention. Clutter distracts the eye, which distracts the brain. A messy desktop (both physical and on the computer) is full of distractions.

Spend a few minutes cleaning up your desk. Personally, I find it very difficult to clean my desk, so I've developed an office cleaning mantra:

> When in doubt, throw it out.

I then follow this three-step plan:

1. File the things that can be filed.
2. Take the unfinished items and put them in a stack to be done soon.
3. Put all the remaining stuff in a large envelope marked, "If I haven't opened this three months from now, I can throw it out." Then seal the envelope.

Three months from now it will take extreme willpower to throw out the envelope without looking at the contents. The point is that I don't spend a lot of time thinking about each item and worrying that I might need it later. When deciding to throw out the envelope I repeat the following mantra:

> When in doubt, throw it out. If I ever do need it, I can ask the source for a copy.

I've also found it useful to take down posters, calendars, and other things that are in my direct line of vision. I still have many posters, they just aren't in my direct view. When I'm sitting at my desk facing my computer, I want blank walls, nothing distracting.

Finally, once you have a visually uncluttered work environment, do the same for your computer. Remove icons from your desktop; turn off all instant messenger clients, music players, stock tickers, and news tickers; and close your email program. I'm an email addict, and if I know I have new email, I read it. I could spend my whole day just waiting for the next email message. Instead, it's much better to open your email program every two to three hours, read everything, and close the program. I don't worry about missing urgent messages. If it is so urgent that the world will end, I'm sure someone will walk by my office and tell me (or perhaps I'll see a vision telling me what to do).

Two things that have added to my productivity: a significant reduction in playing computer games and staying off IM when I need to get work done.

—Victor Raymond
http://www.livejournal.com/
users/badger2305

Spend a few minutes right now doing all these things.

No, really, stop reading and do them. I promise you this book will be here when you're done. I know you like the things that distract you and hate to see them go. They like you, too. That's why they are always popping up and saying, "Look at me! Look at me!" Get rid of them.

 Don Aslett has written a number of books about getting rid of clutter both in the home and in the office. My favorite is *Clutter's Last Stand: It's Time to De-Junk Your Life!* (Adams Media Corporation). The advice is very practical and his writing style is often hilarious.

I've met people who say they work better with a lot of distractions, like having a TV or radio playing in the background. When we're younger and don't care as much about discipline, having a lot of distractions doesn't seem like as much of a problem. We also have fewer responsibilities and deadlines, plus less pressure to get things done. As we get older our needs change, and the environment we're comfortable working in changes, too. Try decluttering your work environment for one week and see if it helps. It may jolt you out of habits developed when you were, essentially, a different person.

Multitasking

System administration is a job where multitasking is the norm. We are downloading the new ISOs of our favorite Linux distro while restoring a file from a backup tape, and reading email while responding to an IM; meanwhile, we have 15 open windows each doing something different. We rock!

This is a good thing. If it is going to take an hour to download an ISO image, the best use of our time is to start it, then do something else. Once the download starts successfully, it doesn't need our attention. We can check back on it later.

The problem is that sometimes we overextend ourselves. We get confused. We make mistakes and have to make a detour to fix the problems we've caused. I've also watched system administrators with so many open windows that they spent more time finding the right window to perform a task than doing the work in that window.

Here are some tricks that help me:

- **Be aware of which tasks to multitask and which not to.** Good tasks to multitask are "hurry up and wait" tasks, such as downloading a large file, compiling a large program, or waiting for a long backup or restore to complete. Anything else shouldn't be multitasked. Do one task at a time well rather than many things at once poorly. Give the top priority your undivided attention. To make sure you don't forget to return to the other tasks, record them in your to do list (see Chapter 5).

- **Be aware of your stress and sleep level.** If you are tired or under a lot of stress, multitask less. There are days when I'm tired, in a bad mood, and very frustrated. Suddenly I realize that I'm working on so many things at once that I'm not getting anything done. I shut down all my windows, my IMs, my iTunes, and so on. I take a deep breath. Then I pick the one thing that is my top priority and do it with no other multitasking. It feels so good.

- **Organize your windows with a virtual window manager.** Rather than have 50 windows open on one screen, a virtual window manager lets you group windows into screens. For example, I might have six virtual screens. One I use for reading email, another is for monitoring my systems, and still another is where I work on issues in our request tracking system, and so on. Rather than having all those windows cluttering one screen, they are well-organized and out of the way when I'm not working in them.

- **Organize your windows the same way every time.** You'll spend less time searching for the right window, and reduce the risk of typing a command into the wrong window, if you always arrange the windows on your screen (or virtual screens) in the same way. For example:

  - When comparing two versions of the same document, I always put the window displaying the older version on the left and the newer version's window on the right.

  - I once worked with machines in London that have failover pairs in the United States. I always put the London window on the right (my reasoning was a mnemonic: London is east of the United States).

  - When writing Perl code, I always use the same three window arrangements: a text editor (wide window, top left), the place where I run/test the program and/or prepare input (narrow window, top right), and the place where I review the output (wide window across the bottom).

- When I am viewing log files of multiple machines to see their combined interaction, I always place the windows in the order that the data is flowing (top to bottom).
- **Use windows to make a nice work space.** Command (shell) windows are free, so don't be stingy. It drives me crazy to see a junior system administrator who uses too few windows. A common example is on Unix or Linux systems when one is debugging an email problem. I've witnessed junior admins who send a test message, then try to type the command to display the tail of the email log file quickly enough to catch the lines related to their test message. Then they display whether the email was delivered properly, which scrolls the log off the top of the window, losing critical information. Then they edit the configuration, save the file, exit, and send a new test message. Stop the insanity! Don't just dive in, prepare your workspace. Create four windows:
  - A wide one that runs tail -f /var/log/mail.log to display the log-file in real time, printing more lines as they appear in the log. Just let that run while performing the other steps.
  - A small window that has the command echo test | mail -s test *testuser@example.com.* You will use command history to repeat that command over and over every time you need to send a test message.
  - The next window will be where you edit the mail system's configuration file. You will save the file, but don't exit the editor. Leave it running.
  - The last window is where you check to see whether the email arrived.

Now you can see all the related displays at the same time, which makes it easier to do your job. You can shift between the various facets of what you are doing by moving your eyes, not typing commands. Much better.

Peak Time for Focus

Some people find it easier to focus at certain times of the day. Part of creating an environment to encourage focus is figuring out the best time to be focused, i.e., when it takes the least amount of effort for you to stay focused. When I schedule mental activity for my peak focus time it feels like I've switched to my "big brain." Take a moment to think about the different parts of the day. Do you find your brain works better in the morning? Mid-morning? After lunch? Afternoon? Late afternoon? At night? Rarely do technical people call themselves "morning people," but that might be unrelated to your ability to focus once you are out of bed.

Your peak time for physical activity may be different than your peak time for mental activity. If you're like me, you feel sleepy after eating lunch and find yourself nodding at your workstation and unable to maintain focus. Take advantage of what would otherwise be a "down" mental period and spend this time doing physical work, such as installing new hardware in a rack or running cables.

Once you've determined your peak focus time, how can you use it to your best advantage? Rearrange your day so that you work on projects during peak time. If you have a regularly scheduled meeting during that time, move it. Don't use peak time to catch up with email or make phone calls. Those might be important tasks, but they don't require your big brain. (In Chapter 5, I discuss more about planning your day.)

The First-Hour Rule

The *first-hour rule* is that the first hour of the workday is usually the quietest hour in an office. I'm not a morning person, but if I can drag myself into work early, I can get much more done in the first hour than during the entire rest of the day because of the lack of interruptions.

How do you spend the first hour of the day? I bet you spend it catching up with email and voice mail. Instead of letting these tasks consume your first hour, why not check your email for subject lines that look important (or email that's from your boss), read those, and then shut off your email reader. Now spend that first hour on a project. You won't have nearly as many interruptions, and the email will be there when you're done. Besides, if you go in really early, no one is in the office to read any of your responses, so what's the rush?

If you have a network monitoring system (and you should) you can check the dashboard view and then be confident that everything is OK and you don't have to look for more detailed system status information. For example, I use the open source program Nagios (*http://www.nagios.org*) to monitor the services I'm responsible for, such as email servers, routers, web servers, etc. When I arrive in the morning, I can look at the summary page and see that all indicators are green and be confident that I can spend my first hour on projects, not worrying that something's down and I don't know it. I started my Nagios configuration very small, just monitoring whether a certain router was up and whether the SMTP port was answering on our email server. From there I grew the configuration as each outage helped me find something else that should be monitored. (More information about Nagios can be found in O'Reilly's *Essential System Administration*.)

If the first hour rule works well for you, turn it into the first two hours rule by coming to the office an hour earlier.

Amusement Park Time Management

Let's apply the first hour strategy to amusement parks. An amusement park ride typically lasts four minutes, and it takes about a minute to walk to the next one. That's five minutes per ride. If you didn't have to wait in line, you could ride 12 attractions per hour! If there are 60 rides at a typical amusement park, you could be done in a dizzying five hours. That's the time between breakfast and lunch!

However, the park is usually busy, and if you wait in line for 25 minutes for each ride, you'll only get to ride 2 per hour (25 + 4 + 1 or 30 minutes each ride). At that rate, the same park would take three 10-hour days.

Who has time for that?

If only you could stack the deck and get the whole park almost completely to yourself so there is no waiting. This turns out to be easy! Many parks open an hour earlier than they advertise. If you show up then, you practically have the entire park to yourself. For example, Disneyland varies the opening time throughout the year. There is a phone number to call to find out tomorrow's opening time. Whatever time this says, show up an hour earlier and you'll find the gate is open. It's true!

In that first hour you can go on 20 rides because the park will be essentially empty. As more guests arrive and the lines lengthen over the next couple of hours, you might get to slightly fewer rides. When the lines grow long, eat an early lunch while everyone else wastes time waiting in line. At noon, the ride lines become shorter because everyone (except you) is silly enough to want to eat lunch right at noon. Soon you will have been on every ride you want, and you can spend the evening and night repeating the rides you really enjoyed, or attend the other attractions at the park.

Meanwhile, everyone else will either have to stay three times longer than you or only experience one-third of the park.

Some parks charge for express lane tickets that let you skip to the front of the line. Now that you know the math, you can make a much better decision about whether those tickets are worth the price.

Interruptions

Interruptions are unavoidable. They are a natural part of the business flow. It is up to us to manage them well.

Being *interrupt driven* means doing tasks as they arrive as opposed to doing tasks based on some business-driven priority scheme. Sure, many times our business directive is to do interruptions as they arrive, but as you advance in your career, I assure you that this will be less and less so. Think about the organizational structure at a retail store. The clerk working the counter is interrupt driven: a customer comes to the counter, the clerk takes his order, makes change, answers questions, and so on. The clerk's boss, on the other hand, has a schedule of things that must be done: she opens the store, orders products, schedules staff, and so on. Yes, the manager stops for interruptions (questions from staff, emergencies, etc.), but that's a fraction of her job.

When we are interrupt driven, we're letting our interrupters manage our time. We're handing control of our workflow to someone else. Now, I'm all in favor of being customer focused, but only you know what your priorities are. If you control when you do tasks, you can intelligently group and prioritize them in ways that save time. For example, you can collect all the tasks in a particular part of the building and do them in a cluster. This reduces the amount of time spent walking up and down between floors. Chapter 8 shows how doing tasks in the order they are requested can be non-optimal and suggests a number of prioritization strategies that will save you time.

Of course, the fastest way to deal with an interruption is to scream, "Get out of my face!" at the requester and slam the door. However, I can't recommend this technique unless you want to get fired. I have met SAs who recommend being gruff, "scary," or even a "bastard operator from hell" to deter customer requests. I think SAs can do better than to follow this advice.

Directing Interruptions Away from You

Let's begin by trying to eliminate the single most annoying interruption that exists: someone interrupting you when he should be going to someone else. Is this the right way to handle such interruptions?

"Tom, there's a problem with the web server."

"Great! I look forward to your results when you talk to the people responsible for the web servers."

No, that would be rude. The great thing about being a system administrator is that everyone assumes that you are all knowing and all powerful. Sadly, most of us are only all powerful within a certain scope of responsibility. While it may be annoying to be asked about systems outside your scope, you really can't get angry at someone for trying. Have you ever *intentionally* asked the wrong person a question? Not likely. So when you get annoyed at someone for making a request that "is obviously not my job," put yourself in that person's shoes. He didn't know a better place to go. Chances are, it's a compliment: you're the smartest person he could think of to ask for help (or the smart people were at lunch). Most organizations don't make it really obvious who is the most appropriate person to go to for help with particular problems.

Until you make it clear who to turn to for help, you can't really get upset that people don't go to the right person. I use several methods to communicate to people the right way to seek help: web pages, signs, email signatures, and so on. When I was at Bell Labs, we had posters all over the walls leading to the SA area that read, "Stop! Have you sent email to 'help'?" At another organization, the first thing I did was to install an internal web site that gave users a list of specialty areas and directed them to the right person given a particular situation. Web browsers were configured to open this page on startup, and soon everyone became familiar with the information on the page.

"Hey, Is There Something Wrong?"

Customers often bother me just to ask, "Hey, do you know that something is wrong?" Having a monitoring system like Nagios that lets them check for themselves can reduce these interruptions. However, if your system is very stable, there are going to be few chances for them to develop the habit of checking the status web page first. The least you can do is to make it a link on your intranet home page.

When someone notices an outage that Nagios hasn't been configured to test, I make a big deal out of thanking him, even going so far as to send a follow-up email pointing out that that situation is now being tested for in Nagios and that we appreciate him making us aware of the issue because it has enabled us to improve our monitoring system.

How do you advertise the right way to get help? Stop for a moment and look around your office. Walk 50 feet from your desk. Now turn and walk back toward your desk while pretending to be a typical user and see what she sees. Does the path naturally lead her to interrupt you or someone else? What can be done to guide the customer to an appropriate person who isn't you? If you have a formal, tiered support system, are customers directed to the right people? How can they be directed better? Maybe a big sign or whiteboard that explains people's responsibilities would prevent a big heap of interruptions. It would be fun to make overhead signs like at an airport, but instead of signs for Concourse A, Baggage Claim, and Ground Transportation, you would hang signs that tell people where to go for help with Email, Internet Outages, and Printers.

Can customers be trained to go to the right place for help? Maybe. The first step is to make sure they're being properly told what to do, then to make sure they get significantly better service when they follow the directions. Punishing someone for not following directions rarely works. Ask any animal trainer and they'll agree: positive reinforcement works better than punishment (in the long term). People not following directions is usually a warning sign that the directions aren't clear to them, aren't visible enough, or that the directions don't work.

Alas, people will still come to you when you are trying to focus, which leads us to the next section.

You Can Say "Go Away" Without Being a Jerk

When someone interrupts us, how do we tell him to go away without sounding like a jerk? The key is to acknowledge their request respectfully.

As discussed in the previous chapter, there are times when our job is to be the interrupt catcher, the person fielding interruptions so that other SAs can focus on projects. However, there are times when we are in designated "project time" and need to stay focused. What do we do when interrupted during those times?

First, it's important to understand what customers expect of us. *Fundamentally, customers will be satisfied if they feel they have been acknowledged.* You don't have to fix their problem for them to be acknowledged. They just need to feel that they've been heard and get confirmation that their request will be completed.

When someone stops by my office and asks me to do something that I'm going to put off until later, I make sure he feels acknowledged both verbally and visually. First, I say, "I understand your issue. Let me write it down so I don't forget it." Then I write down his request as he watches. I say what I write as I'm writing it. It usually sounds like, "[Person] needs [such and such] by [date]." Then I turn to him and ask, "Did I capture that right?"

When he says "yes," it gives closure to the issue. Having achieved closure, he usually leaves on his own, if I don't ruin it by saying something to continue the conversation. I've found it best to say "Thank you," while giving a nod. Anything else just reopens the dialog. Closure makes it difficult for them to start to push for immediate action. If he does push for immediate action, then I know I have misunderstood the urgency of his request, and we can discuss the time requirements. But now, I'm driving the conversation, which means I'm in the position of power during negotiations.

Automated systems need to acknowledge people, too. When customers send email to a request-tracking system, they should receive an autoreply with the issue's ID number. If they submit an issue through a web-based system, they should immediately be able to view the issue status so they can be confident that it actually is in the database. People hate to feel they are submitting a request to a black hole. A personal response is wonderful but unrealistic. An automated response acknowledging the receipt of the request is sufficient. No response keeps customers in suspense and is unfair. Lack of response is one reason why I don't like to submit bug reports to certain vendors. It's very trendy to have software automatically submit a bug report when it crashes. Netscape has FullCircle, Microsoft has their feedback agent, and Apple Mac OS X has something similar. They all leave me dissatisfied because I never receive any kind of acknowledgment. I have no way of knowing that it's not just some kind of feel-good hoax set up to make customers think the vendor cares while they actually discard the submissions. I don't expect to receive a phone call from a product manager saying, "Hey, remember that crash you had last week? Thanks for submitting the report! We've fixed it and named you Customer of the Month!" However, it would be nice to receive email to acknowledge the submission. (I should note that when Tom Reingold was at Bell Labs, he not only called and congratulated the submitter of every 1,000th request, he took them to lunch and used it as an opportunity to ask them how they would like to see service improved. So there!)

Sure, all customers want their requests completed, but you can't always get what you want, and everyone knows it. However, if people don't feel acknowledged, they won't be happy. At worst they will feel ignored; at best they will assume you aren't doing something when you are.

Don't customers want everything right now? No. I believe that customers know, deep down, that they can't always get that. If they ask you to order a new PC, they expect the request to be acknowledged, but they know that even with overnight shipping, they're not going to be able to stand in your office waiting for it to arrive. They will be satisfied with an acknowledgment and a date on which they can expect the order to arrive.

Customers Want to See Action More Than They Want to Receive Action

Once I was in my office and a customer rushed in.

"Server XYZ is down!" he said, in a panic.

"I'm on it!" I replied.

I turned to my workstation, typing occasionally. From what the customer could see, it seemed like I had simply returned to my work and was completely ignoring his panicked request.

This was in the early days of remote serial console or long-haul KVM switches. I was actually hard at work fixing the problem, but visually the customer wasn't seeing me do anything different than when he arrived.

He became upset. The customer's expectation for "fixing a down server" involved me jumping up, running down the hall, fiddling with the funny combination lock on the machine room, then laying hands on the server. Because I wasn't meeting his expectations, he expressed his dissatisfaction in rather colorful language. He thought I was just going to sit there and do nothing to see if the server came up on its own. I was able to clear up the confusion by showing him what was on my screen.

When this happens now, I assume that the customer does not know about console servers and long-haul KVM switches. First, I verify that the server is down while I announce what test I'm doing. "Let's try pinging it!" I announce. "I can't reach it." But then instead of dashing off to the data center, I say something like, "Hey, have you seen this? I can access the console remotely as if I'm in the computer room!" I turn the monitor so the customer can see what I'm doing, show off the technology a little, and then go to work fixing the problem.

Soon they get bored and go away, satisfied that I'm working on the problem.

My little demo slows me down a bit, but it is still faster than actually walking to the computer room, and the customer is much more satisfied because he receives visual proof that I'm attending to his request.

"Bored but satisfied" is so much better than "panicked and impatiently waiting."

Conversely, customers will be the least satisfied if they *feel* ignored. This has nothing to do with whether they really are being ignored. If you start working on their request but they don't know you have, they will assume you haven't. That sucks, but it's true.

Hopefully I've convinced you that acknowledgment is important, and managing your time based on your priorities is important. So how do we combine the two? By using the process of delegate, record, or do.

That leads us to the next section.

Delegate, Record, or Do

When someone interrupts you with a request during your designated project time, you have a few options:

- **Delegate it.** If someone else can do it, delegate it to him.
- **Record it.** If only you can do the request, but it isn't urgent, record the request. Be sure to do so in a way that the customer trusts; don't just promise to remember it.
- **Do it.** If the request is truly urgent, such as a service outage, drop what you are working on and do the request.

I admit that I actually pause to think, "Delegate, record, or do." It helps me focus on what I'm going to do with this person who is, alas, breaking my focus. The following sections provide more detail about this process.

Delegate it

If you have set up a mutual interruption shield as discussed in the opening of Chapter 1, you can refer the person to your shield partner. You don't have to say, "I'm sorry, but this is my project time, so I'm going to shove you on someone else." You can say it very politely.

Since people need a visual, positive confirmation that they've been heard and taken seriously, I think the best technique is to pick up the phone and call your shield partner to delegate the request while the customer watches. People don't want to have to re-explain themselves to each person they get delegated to, so I always try to explain the issue to the delegate. I can often explain it in technical terms, which is more efficient than the customer's original request.

Here's the general form: I say out loud, "Ah, let me ask Mary to do this" (I pick up the phone and dial Mary). "Hi, Mary. Joe is here. He needs X and Y. I'm sending him over to you." I look at the customer and say, "Stop by Mary's office, and she'll help you." Now Joe has received excellent acknowledgement of his request, and Mary is prepared to handle the task.

As technically inclined people, we often forget what it's like to be a nontechnical customer making a request. It may have been difficult, and possibly scary, to figure out how to phrase the request, so taking the time to explain it to Mary in your language makes it easier for Joe.

Sometimes the request is rather complicated, and I don't want to risk the miscommunication I can introduce by repeating a request incorrectly. However, I can still help focus the issue. For example, "Hi, Mary. Joe is here. He has a rather complicated request related to the web server. I'm going to send him over to you right now."

Of course, there are times when you are in a hurry and just can't call Mary. I think it is obnoxious to answer a request with a question like, "Did you talk with Mary?" A better way to express this is to simply say, "Mary is on call right now. Could you speak to her about this?" It sounds more official and orderly. People find a certain comfort to following an official process.

If your coworker says she doesn't know how to do the task you are trying to delegate to her, you have a few different options. You can use this as an opportunity to teach her how to do the task. That way, she'll know how to do it in the future. Otherwise, you might ask the customer if the task can wait—if it can, record it.

Record it

If the task can wait, you can record it for later action. Record it in a place where it won't get lost. Make sure the customer sees you record the request so that he has visible confirmation that he isn't being ignored.

If you use The Cycle System, as described in Chapter 5, enter the request into your to do list. This is appropriate for smaller tasks that will be done soon.

For larger tasks, my favorite place to record a request is in a request-tracker application. I've found that the open source tool RT by Best Practical (*http:// www.BestPractical.com*) is better than a lot of the commercial systems around. (O'Reilly recently published a book called *RT Essentials* that covers all the details of configuring, administrating, and using RT.) Emailing to RT automatically starts a new issue to track. If you haven't set up RT yet, a poor man's alternative is to email yourself the request. While you're at it, email yourself a reminder to install RT.

To make sure that the customer sees me taking action, I say out loud, "Let me record this in my to do list so I don't forget," or "Let me create an RT entry." Then as you type the message, speak what you are typing. "Jill needs a new printer installed. It is in the box just inside her office. She needs it by this Thursday at 9 a.m."

 Always record a time in your deadline. A Thursday deadline can lead to trouble when a customer assumes you meant Thursday morning, but you actually meant Thursday close of business.

I then turn to the customer, who has heard what I've typed, and say, "Anything else I should capture?" This helps eliminate miscommunication. It also gives them the satisfaction of thinking that they're in control—which they are, sort of.

After clicking submit, send, or whatever the software requires, say something reassuring like, "I got it!" and return to the work you were doing before you were interrupted. Recording the request in RT, a PDA, or a to do list system shows professionalism that is reassuring to your customer. Writing on little scraps of paper or 3M Post-it Notes has the opposite effect.

Never try to remember the item in your brain only. I've already discussed keeping the front part of your brain free for more important things. Don't try to remember the customer's request. You're a smart person (and good-looking, too), but don't trust your brain to do something that paper can do better. Record it, then let it go. Free your brain. Which leads us to....

The Hallway Ambush

When someone stops me in the hallway and asks me to do something, I record it in my to do list. However, if I am without my organizer, I would rather refuse to acknowledge the request than trust my brain to remember it. I'm honest but blunt. I say something like, "OK, so I agree that's the best course of action. However, I'm in the middle of something, and I don't have my PDA with me. I don't want to risk forgetting this. Could you do me a favor and email me the words 'install web monkey' and that will jog my memory." By giving the person the exact words to use, the task becomes less of a burden on her. However, this tactic also unburdens your brain from having to remember the exact request.

If this situation happens while I'm near a computer that can send email, I'll ask the person at the computer to email me the reminder, even if they weren't part of the conversation!

Oh, and that reminds me. How dare you go somewhere without your PDA/PAA! Always keep it with you.

Do it

The third option is to do the request immediately. Your focus will be lost, but at least you made two good attempts to first deflect the task. If a request should take less than two minutes, it can be less work to do it than to record it and pick it up later.

Of course, if the issue is an emergency or a major outage, there's no other good choice. Heck, the major outage might also affect you, so it's worth doing right away.

I highly recommend that your organization create its own definition of *major outage*. This can give newer SAs direction and guidance, and if it's stated on your policy web site, it can set expectations with your customers. For example, a LAN group I worked with once defined a major outage to be any outage affecting more than 10 people. Other businesses define a major outage based on whether a deadline is in jeopardy or a Service Level Agreement (SLA) will be missed.

Before you do the customer's request, take a moment to record where you left off, or at least save your work. That makes it easier to return to the task. It also helps you focus on the new task because your brain isn't cluttered with trying to remember where you left off.

Summary

- Focus is important. You gain focus by removing distractions and dealing efficiently with interruptions.
- Interruptions are, essentially, someone else controlling your time. Interruptions are the natural enemy of focus, and, therefore, time management.
- Interruptions are bad because they delay your current work but also because returning to the prior task can lead to errors. Fixing those errors can take more time than the original task.
- Removing distractions helps you to keep focus: clean your desk and your computer desktop, and remove distractions from your office. Disable IM, new email notifiers, and so on.
- Everyone has a different peak time for mental and physical activity. Discover yours, and then schedule appropriate tasks for those times.
- The first hour of the day can be your most productive, since it has the fewest interruptions. Getting to work slightly earlier than coworkers increases this productive time. Don't waste that time with maintenance tasks; use it for important projects.

Some General Advice

Sadly, this book can't give much advice about how to do the task. I don't even know what operating system you are using. I can, however, give you these general recommendations:

- **Measure twice, cut once.** Be extra sure before you make a change you can't undo.
- **Make a backup before you change a file.** Having a backup of a file can get you out of trouble. However, this only works if you make the backup first!
- **If all else fails, read the manual.** When you can't figure out the solution, try the resources that you often forget to access.
- **When debugging, change one thing at a time.** By changing one thing at a time, you see which change actually affected the system. This avoids confusion as the debugging process proceeds.
- **Always test your work.** Some people never seem to make mistakes. I find that they are the people who do a lot of testing—we just don't see it.
- **You aren't done until your customer tests it, too.** You may think you've tested things sufficiently, but until the customer has done his own tests, you really don't know whether you've fixed his problem.
- **The strangest problems often turn out to be misconfigured DNS.** DNS is critical to so many subsystems, often in obscure ways, that a problem with DNS can mask itself as other problems. This goes for a client that can't reach its DNS servers, as well as a host with invalid DNS data describing it, or a client trying to reach a host with invalid DNS data.

- The delegate, record, or do process permits you to take back control of your time. Use this when your project work is interrupted. *Delegating* the task means handing it off to someone else. *Recording* the task lets you acknowledge the request, but schedule it for later. *Doing* the task is your last resort, but it should be used for emergencies and outages.
- When you record it, you gain the ability to plan and schedule rather than being interrupt driven. This is something we discuss further in Chapter 8.
- When you acknowledge a request, you should do it in a visually meaningful way. Make sure the person sees you record it, and confirm it with her.

- Customers would rather have a request acknowledged than not know whether it was received, even if this means the request is being delayed.

- Request-tracking systems like RT let you record requests in a central database that other system administrators can access and that customers can use to check a request's status.

- Never trust your brain to remember a request. Record the request on paper or digitally. Your brain has better things to do.

Just Start

Once you get started, it won't be as difficult as you thought. In fact, often we don't begin a task because we make excuses about how much time something will take, but once we get started, we find out that the task is relatively quick.

A friend who promised to give me feedback on chapters of this book as they were written was weeks late with her notes on Chapter 1. She kept putting off getting started because she told herself she couldn't start until she found a full two-hour block to do a really good job. It turned out that Chapter 1 was less than 10 pages and only required about a half-hour to review.

If she had just started—instead of making up rules about when she could start—she would have been done much sooner.

CHAPTER 3
Routines

The term "routine" has a bad reputation. How many times have you seen advertisements for products that promise to "get you out of that old routine" or refer to a "boring routine?" Boring is bad, right?

No! As a system administrator I crave boredom. I want an entire week when things happen on schedule, projects get done on time, software installs without trouble, and documentation gives me the right answer. "Give me just one boring day!" I shout when a big server crashes or a customer comes to me with an impossible but urgent request.

What I wouldn't give for an entire boring month!

There are technical means to improve the situation. We can make things more boring (in a good way!) through long-term planning and suitable infrastructure that makes things run smoother. For example: automating new machine installation so that every host starts out the same, controlling and enforcing updates so all hosts stay in sync, keeping security infrastructure in place so that it is ubiquitous and less burdensome, and so on. There are books about those topics already—I happen to prefer *The Practice of System and Network Administration* (Addison Wesley).

I don't want to make system administration 100 percent boring—I don't think that's actually possible. As long as there are new software packages to try or new hardware platforms to explore, there will always be plenty of fun in system administration.

There will also be a certain amount of chaos. System administration deals with the real world, and the real world is full of chaos.

However, I do want to eliminate the frustrating chaos that keeps me from having fun. Here's a little something about routines to keep in mind:

> Routines give us a way to think once, do many.

Programmers figured this out a long time ago. They reuse code libraries rather than reinventing every new feature every time. Why reinvent the print function for each program you write? Sure, C's printf function isn't the most efficient way to print formatted data, but imagine how crazy (and inefficient) it would be if every program ever written reinvented a way to print data.

Routines are very powerful because they enable us to think less, reserving brain cycles for more important tasks. This is similar to saving brainpower by writing down our appointments and to do items instead of trying to memorize them.

USER FRIENDLY by Illiad

Sample Routines

We can do the same thing in time management: develop routines whenever possible. Here are some examples.

Routine #1: Gas Up on Sunday

I refill my car's gas tank every Sunday. It's a routine I've developed, and it has served me well.

It all started when I realized that I'm often late to work on Monday morning, and I'm doubly late when I realize that I don't have enough gas to get to the office. I tried to get out of the house earlier on Mondays but that failed. Finally, I realized that it would be smart of me to fill up on Sunday so it was one less thing to do on Monday morning. It worked.

I used to procrastinate about filling my gas tank. As a result, there was a little extra chaos in my life, as random appointments would be delayed by my need to stop for gas.

I didn't just procrastinate, I fretted! "Should I get gas now? I think I can make it." "Gosh, I'm running behind; maybe I'll get gas tomorrow. I'm sure I'll remember to leave the house early." "Oh, I was going to get gas last night, but I was so tired I forgot. Oh, damn." A lot of brain energy spent on something so simple.

Now that kind of chaos is eliminated from the first half of my week—sometimes the whole week if I don't do much driving.

It's a nice, simple routing that works for me.

The part of my brain that actively thinks about things had one less thing to think about (getting gas), and soon the habit was in the automatic part of my brain. When I'm driving on Sunday, I fill my gas tank.

The key to a good routine is that with enough practice you start doing it without having to think about it. Less thinking about gas means more brainpower left over for other things. Eventually, you might actually forget why you established the routine. That's OK. In fact, it's a good thing. You don't have to think about breathing; it's an autonomic function of the brain. Imagine how distracted you would be if every few seconds you had to stop, recall why breathing is important, decide to breathe, then concentrate to move your muscles to inhale and exhale!

One Sunday I was filling up my tank, and I mentioned to my passenger that I always get gas on Sunday. He asked me why, and I couldn't remember. I just knew that I had been doing it for a long time, that I started doing it to correct a problem, and that it had successfully solved the problem for nearly a decade.

Wow! Talk about autonomic! It took me a minute or two to remember the original reason. How cool would it be if other things in our life that we fret about became automatic functions?

Routine #2: Always Bring My Organizer

In theory, I want my organizer wherever I might need it. I know I need it at work. That's obvious. I sometimes need it at home. Should I leave it at work if I don't think I'll need it at home that evening? Should I leave it in my car or take it into the house? "Nah, I'll leave it here. I won't need it tonight."

Then it turns out that I do need it, and since I'm too lazy to go out to my car, I agree to Thursday night dinner with friends, as I don't recall any conflicts with that date. I then either miss the appointment (since I didn't record it), or it turns out that I do have a conflict and I have to reschedule, which creates a lot of work for me and all the other people involved.

Is rescheduling more work than running out to my car to get the darn organizer? Of course. But I don't go to the car because when I'm in the moment, it feels like less work to try to remember the appointment. I want the easier option that exists right now, not in some theoretical future when I might be wrong. Look at me! I just saved a trip to the car!

A worse scenario is when I get into my car in the morning to drive to work and find I don't have my organizer with me. I think, "Where is it? Well, it's not here. Did I bring it home? I don't know. I must have left it at work."

Of course, when I get to work I discover that my organizer actually was at home. Now I have to spend the day without it. To do list items get confused, appointments are missed—it's awful.

To help me develop this routine I found an excellent mantra to use:

> If I ask "Should I bring my organizer?" the answer is "Yes."

That has a domino effect that works well. When I'm leaving work, I know to take my organizer. When I'm leaving for work, if my organizer isn't in my car, I know I have to go into the house to find it. Since I always take it with me, I know I couldn't possibly have left it at work the night before.

This is why in 14 years I've lost my organizer only once. Every time I leave a room, go home from work, get into a car, get out of a car—everywhere I go—I know I should have my organizer in my hand. Because of this absolute consistency, the habit was able to develop very quickly and indelibly in my mind. Sometimes we misplace things because we lose track of them. We put an item down, and later we leave the room without it because we aren't in the habit of taking it with us all the time. Because we don't always have our organizer with us, our brain rationalizes that it's OK that we don't have it with us *right now*. I have developed a habit, almost a tactile addiction, to having that organizer in my hand.

 The one time I lost my organizer I was in a rush and was distracted by having to carry many things at once. I would like to point out that the limo company returned my organizer by overnight air the next day. I was very lucky.

What are the things that you find yourself without? Why don't you carry them with you all the time?

Take a moment to consider the following items that might be easier to always have with you than to waste brainpower on deciding whether you should bring them along:

- Your PDA or PAA
- Your cell phone and/or pager
- A pen
- Your wallet, purse, etc.
- ID cards
- Keys (metal and electronic)
- Your medical ID cards, insurance information, etc.
- A laptop (for some people)

Oh, sure, let them laugh at you for wearing a pocket protector. We know the value of always having a pen on hand.

Routine #3: Regularly Meet with My Boss

I need "face time" with my boss. I like to be independent, but that has its limits. Scheduling meetings with my boss is a major time investment. If I add up all the bits of time I spend Instant Messaging her, talking to her secretary, and so on, it can take me 30 minutes to arrange for 15 minutes of time with my boss. That's just crazy.

So instead, we've agreed to meet or speak on the phone every Tuesday at 10 a.m., whether we need to or not. Now that 15 minutes takes zero time to arrange.

You might want to do something similar with your boss, especially if you don't feel you get to talk with your boss enough. Five minutes of status updates every day at 9 a.m. can be more useful to you, and less annoying to him, than grabbing him throughout the day.

Oddly enough, this also helps if your boss says you require too much of his attention. If half your attempts to see your boss are just to schedule time for larger discussions, it might be better to have a regularly scheduled meeting time with him. It consolidates the meetings.

Routine #4: The Check-In-with-Staff Walk-Around

There was a time at Bell Labs when I managed 15 other system administrators. I wanted to be a hands-off manager—the other SAs were all smart, hardworking, and independent. I mostly left everyone alone. However, I soon learned that they felt ignored. I needed to spend more time with them.

If You Have to Ask, the Answer Is "Yes"

Over the years, I've decided the answer to these questions is always "yes." I can now stop wasting brainpower trying to make a decision each time the issue comes up.

- Would this be a good time to save the file I'm working on?
- Should I take my organizer with me (versus leaving it here)?
- Should I add this to my to do list?
- Should I check my calendar before I agree to this appointment?
- Should I write this on my calendar?
- Should I check to see whether I have plans after work before I agree to stay late?
- Should I check to see whether I have any early appointments before I decide to play one more game of *Half Life* this morning?
- Should I do The Cycle today (versus slacking off)?
- Should I fill my car's gas tank now (versus procrastinating until it is an emergency)?
- Should I do this small task or chore now (versus procrastinating and hoping nobody notices or the task doesn't turn into an emergency)?

The answer to all of these questions is "yes." This list was developed over 10 painful years of getting into trouble (in small and big ways) by thinking about the question, weighing the benefits of both choices, and making a thoughtful but wrong decision. I was trying to be smart. It took me a long time to realize, "Stop thinking! The answer is 'yes!'" Don't weigh the issues; don't waste brainpower making a decision; don't convince yourself that just this one time things will be different! If you have to ask yourself the question, the answer is "Yes!"

In most cases, it takes longer to make a decision about a task than to do the task. Opening up my PDA and checking my calendar takes 10 seconds, but I can spend just as much time rationalizing that today my memory is good enough to not need to check.

Many of those questions are equivalent to asking, "Should I trust my memory or my organizer's memory?" We already know that our memory is faulty; otherwise, we wouldn't be using an organizer, right? Use it!

It took me nearly 10 years to develop a rule for each of those questions, and, by amazing coincidence, for each of them the answer was the same. Save yourself many painful experiences and believe me: the answer is "Yes!"

However, scheduling mini meetings with 15 people would have taken longer than the meetings themselves and wouldn't have worked in the chaotic environment of system administration. Therefore, every Monday and Thursday at 9 a.m., I would do my "walk-around." I would walk a particular path that went by each person's office. Their offices were, essentially, in three different clusters, so it was almost like having three mini status meetings. I would stop in, say "hello," and this would present them with an opportunity to bring up issues.

It would take me half a day to do this, but it was a really good opportunity to troubleshoot problems in real time, remove roadblocks, and solve the problem of people feeling ignored.

Our weekly staff meeting was on Tuesday morning. The Monday walk-around usually resolved a lot of issues that would normally tie up the Tuesday meeting, so we reduced the time allotted to our staff meetings. Shorter meetings are cool.

I was surprised at how well it worked. I was also surprised that anyone noticed. Alas, one day I was walking towards a cluster of offices, and I overheard someone saying, "Here comes Tom for his Thursday visit," followed by a little laughter.

OK, they were mocking me. Did I change? Did I vary the schedule to be less predictable and obvious? No. I'm too thickheaded for that.

However, I did notice that over time my staff started planning their schedule around my walks. Sometimes I would arrive and they'd have a list of issues on the whiteboard ready to discuss.

Here are two takeaways from this story:

- Develop a routine that solves your problems.
- Perform the routine on a predictable schedule, and others will plan their schedules around you.

Routine #5: The Check-In-with-Customers Walk-Around

If you are supporting a number of people who are in the same building as you, you can increase customer satisfaction by doing a walk-around once a day to visit customers, talk with them, answer questions, fix problems as you see them, record bigger problems to be worked on later, and so on. If anything, it develops a better rapport with your customers. That alone is very valuable.

One person I worked with had a very shy, smart, but not so computer-savvy group of customers. They had a tendency to not report problems because of their shyness, and possibly because the previous system administrator was a bit of a grouch. As a result, they were living with many inefficient work-arounds—most of which my coworker could easily fix to make their lives better.

When I learned that my coworker was doing a daily walk-around to trouble-shoot problems, I was appalled! Doing this went against our policy of recording all issues in our request-tracking system! It was an affront to our attempts to get people to send email to "help" to report problems. How could this be a good thing?

I soon learned that it was a great thing. People tend to not report little annoyances, figuring that the problems can't be fixed (especially people who aren't computer-savvy). The walk-arounds dramatically reduced the number of annoyances and greatly increased the group's productivity. It also helped foster a better relationship between my coworker and her customers, so much so that they began to include her in planning for major projects, which increased her ability to solve problems before they happened.

Do not use this technique if you have a problem saying no to people. Part of the reason it worked so well was that my coworker employed something like the delegate, record, do process of Chapter 2. I'll call her system *fix, redirect, or sympathize*.

- **Fix.** If the problem was easy to fix (less than two minutes), she'd fix it right then and there.

- **Redirect.** If the problem couldn't be fixed in a few minutes, she would help the customer send email to "help" to create a ticket in the request-tracking system. This was a group that wasn't used to creating tickets, so it was scary for them. Walking them through the process made it less intimidating.

- **Sympathize.** Many times the issue was just something that couldn't be fixed, or it was a known problem that wouldn't be fixed for a while. My coworker found that the best thing to do was to show sympathy without being condescending. "Yeah," she would sigh, "it's crummy that it works that way." The person would agree and feel better now that their complaint was acknowledged. Then my coworker would say, "I don't think there's a way around that, but I'll keep an ear out for a solution." This benefited the customer in that it validated that something was annoying and unfixable, rather than leaving it a mystery. It benefited my coworker in that it prevented the unsolvable requests from entering the request-tracking system but gave her a way to gain an understanding of what the general issues were. Some were noted in her PDA. When she did learn of a solution, she could return to the customer with the solution and look like a miracle worker.

The important thing is that she didn't try to solve every problem right then and there. Sometimes the walk-around was a more efficient way to collect requests that would be done later. Other times she was developing relationships with customers that would help her understand those customers' long-term needs. Other times it was simply a way to offer sympathy to get people beyond the unsolvable problems of our world.

I imagine that when my coworker started using the walk-around technique, she was overwhelmed by how many issues were being reported. As I mentioned, do not employ this technique if you have a problem saying no to customers. This technique requires discipline, or you'll end up spending the entire day with the first person you talk with. However, over time, the initial flood of requests will be dealt with, and the walk-around can become more of a maintenance mode kind of thing.

Routine #6: Pre-Compile Manual Backup-Tape Changes

In the Preface, I told an anecdote about changing the backup tapes. It was a complicated task with eight different tape servers that may or may not have needed a fresh tape each day. Each day I would spend time calculating which tapes were full enough to warrant a new tape (i.e., the next night's backups wouldn't fit in the remaining free tape). Then I would walk around to all eight servers, scattered all over the building, with the new tapes.

Eventually, I realized that I could avoid all the calculations if I changed the "big servers" every day and the "little servers" once or twice a week. That was a big savings, not just in my time but in my brain resources.

Again, this was a case of "stop thinking, just do." Sure, I wasted some tape by estimating rather than doing a perfect job, but my time was more valuable than the tape.

The other part of the story is that I tended to change the tapes at the end of the day. If I was deeply involved in a project (I usually was), then I wouldn't realize how late it was and would be scrambling to change the tapes. Usually I would be late to leave work, and the need to change the tapes would just make me later. Whether I was going home after work or to one of my many volunteer responsibilities, I would end up angry and upset because "those darn tapes made me late...again!"

This was a case of needing to figure out a better schedule. I realized this mantra:

> If it has to be done every day, do it early in the day.

After I did my morning planning using The Cycle, I would list "change tapes" as an A priority every day.

As a result, there was one less thing weighing heavy on my mind all day, and I could be more focused and less stressed. I arrived home happier and less late. I started the day feeling like I had accomplished something right off the bat, and I had!

Routine #7: During Outages, Communicate to Management

Once upon a time there was a network outage. To make matters worse, there was miscommunication from the system administrators to management and the customers. Management felt they should have been told earlier about the problem. The system administrators felt they should be left alone to solve the problem. I'm sure this kind of thing has never happened to you...not.

After this event, we decided to develop a routine for the future. After all, this wouldn't be the last outage.

The routine was simple: after an hour, a particular manager (the boss of the chief system administrator) would be notified of an outage, even if it was late at night. The system administrators would then update this person every half hour until the problem was resolved. The manager would notify upper management and customers (if the outage didn't prevent communication to the customers) so the SAs could focus on solving the problem.

It was a simple routine and it worked well. Too bad we didn't have it in place before the first calamity.

If your company is particularly visible (hello Amazon, Google, and Yahoo!), such a routine should involve the Public Relations department. It's important to have this routine worked out before your first major outage, no matter how difficult it is to discuss. Some outages are so big that news reporters will want to know what's going on. You can imagine how messy things can get. This was more common long ago when anything with the words "Internet" or "computer security" was spiffy enough to draw in the news media. (Now the media has become jaded, and "Microsoft security hole affects millions of businesses" is unfortunately no longer considered news.) Nonetheless, if your business is high profile, it is important to have a media strategy worked out with the PR department ahead of time. Know whom to refer to if reporters start calling. If you don't have such a plan in place, the best answer you can give is, "No comment;" then hang up the phone before you are tempted to say anything else. It's very tempting to say something to a reporter, but many system administrators have learned that the best thing to do during an outage is to work on the technical issues and let PR deal with the media.

Routine #8: Use Automatic Checks While Performing Certain Tasks

I've developed the following habit so that I don't lock my keys in the car: when I'm about to close my door, I hold the door with my right hand and squeeze my left hand to make sure I feel my keys in it. Only if I'm holding my keys do I then close the door. I have a similar ritual when leaving my house.

Not that I've locked myself out a lot, but the few times it happened always seemed to be at the worst possible times and took several hours to remedy.

How does this relate to system administration? There are many automatic checks we can introduce into our work:

- When I leave a secured room, I make sure I feel my access card-key in my pocket. (Related rule: I never put my card-key down on a table, floor, whatever, even just for a second. It always goes in my pocket and my pocket is where it goes.)

- When I'm near equipment, I always pause to check for air flow. In particular, I make sure fans are not blocked by cables or other devices.

- Any time a new hire joins the company, I always stop by to introduce myself, welcome her, fix any immediate problems she has, and explain how to get computer help in the future. If I can fix her immediate problems, it can help her get started sooner, and the sooner I can train her to create tickets (rather than call me directly), the better I can manage my time.

- When I see a person I don't recognize, I always smile, stop, introduce myself, and ask for the person's name. I then ask to read it off his ID badge, telling him it will help me to remember it because "I'm a visual learner." New people think I'm being friendly. I'm really checking for trespassers.

- Before I disconnect a network cable I set up a continuous "ping" (one per second), which should start failing when I disconnect the correct cable.

- Every time I add a new rule to my firewall, I first set up a demonstration of what I want to block and show that it isn't blocked. Then I add the firewall rule. Then I repeat the demonstration and show that it now fails. (If I don't do the demo before I add the rule, I can't be sure the rule works for the reason I think it does.)

A More Useful Ping

It can be useful to have ping produce a beep for every successful ping. That way you can be elsewhere in the room disconnecting cables and not have to keep running back to your screen to see whether the pings are working.

Linux *ping* has an -a (audible) switch, which produces a beep.

Solaris and other Unix systems without the -a option can use the following trick. The output of "ping" happens to include a colon only on lines that report success. You simply pass the output through the tr command to translate each colon into a Ctrl-G (the "bell" character).

```
$ ping -s 64.32.179.56 | tr : ^G
```

(Solaris requires the -s option to make it a continuous ping. Others do not.)

To get a Ctrl-G to appear on the command line, you may have to precede it with a Ctrl-V. That is, you type:

```
$ ping -s 64.32.179.56 | tr : CTRL-V CTRL-G
```

Routine #9: Always Back Up a File Before You Edit

When I'm about to edit a configuration file, I always make a backup. I don't waste time thinking, "Gosh, is this file important enough?" If I have to ask, the answer is "Yes." I make backups the same way every time so there is no time wasted figuring out the best way. My system is to copy the file to a file with today's date on it. For example, *named.conf* is copied to *named.conf-20060120* (January 20, 2006). I used to use the file's "last modified" date, but I found that it was much better to use today's date, which leaves a trail of when I made changes. In Unix, I can check the file into an RCS repository, which gives me infinite history of the file's changes (more on that in Chapter 13).

It's tempting to convince yourself, "I'm making a small change that I'll be able to manually undo" or "I'm an expert, I can't mess this up." However, hindsight has found that a backup is better. Especially three weeks from now when you can't figure out why that service has stopped functioning.

Routine #10: Record "To Take" Items for Trips

I travel a lot. I used to forget to bring things, and when I hadn't, I'd still be nervous that I might have forgotten to bring something. Who needs that kind of stress?

Now, I write a "things to pack" list on the righthand side of my to do list for the day I'll be traveling. For weeks (or months) leading up to the trip, anytime I think of something I should bring on the trip I pop open my organizer and write it on that list. Since I always have the organizer with me, I never fail to record an idea.

When I pack, I check off the items as they go into my suitcase.

I also create a second list of the things to have in hand when I leave. That's usually my tickets, my wallet, my suitcases, and so on. I use this list to help me pack the car. If someone else is picking me up, this list includes the items I keep near my front door so they are there when my ride arrives.

I use these lists for both work and nonwork trips. I'd hate to get out of the habit just because I was traveling for pleasure. I reuse these lists to form my next list. I have culled items from past lists to create a master checklist that I keep in my Notes section.

How to Develop Your Own Routines

Now that you've seen some example routines that work for me, how can you develop routines for yourself? Here are some things to look for:

- **Repeated events that aren't scheduled.** Often there is a task or meeting that you repeat many times a week (or month) that isn't scheduled regularly. Would things be helped if it was scheduled in advance? Are you spending more energy scheduling the meeting than preparing for it? If so, develop a schedule. Propose either a regular time and day or a series of dates and times and get agreement up front.

- **Maintenance tasks.** A lot of IT is like gardening: you have to weed a little each week; you can't do all your weeding in a marathon weekend at the beginning of the summer and then not weed for the rest of the season. If it has to be done a little each day, week, or month, make it into a routine. If you are cleaning out a storage room, do an hour of work each day. If you are auditing your user database for people who have left the company, review 100 accounts each day until you are done.

- **Relationships and career networking.** Relationships require maintenance and are also similar to gardening (they grow if you work diligently, starve if they are ignored, and die if they get too much attention). There are four groups of people you need to maintain relationships with: your customers (or your single point of contact for each customer group), your staff (who report to you), your peers, and your boss(es).

Do you routinely touch base with each of them? The key to networking (the career kind, not the data kind) is to maintain relationships throughout the year, not just when you are looking for a new job. Schedule lunch once a month with your mentor or a person who is part of your network.

- **When procrastinating takes longer than action.** If you find yourself spending more time thinking about a task than it would take to do the task, just do it. (Thinking of doing a task is not to be confused with the thinking a task may require.)

- **Things you forget often.** The next time you find yourself in a bind because you forgot something, develop a routine to prevent future occurrences. Hang your keys in the same place each night when you come home, and you'll develop the habit of grabbing them every time you leave. Or, if you must take something with you when you leave, use it to block the door so you'll be sure to see it on your way out. It's important to communicate these routines with your significant other(s). It does no good to always place your wallet and keys on the entrance hall table if your partner is always going to "put them away" somewhere else.

- **Inconsequential or low-priority tasks that can be skipped occasionally but shouldn't be.** There are often tasks that can be skipped once and nothing bad will happen. However, skip them too many times and you're in trouble. This includes things like changing backup tapes, ordering supplies, and so on. Put "order supplies" (or whatever the task is) in your PDA/PAA repeating reminders list for every Monday. It's better to ignore the reminder when there's nothing to order (or do) than to forget to do it at all.

- **Developing new skills.** Some people complain that they never have time for training. Others schedule one training class a year whether they know what it will be or not. It's never going to happen if you don't make it happen.

- **Keeping up-to-date.** It is better to schedule one hour a week of "closed-door time" for magazine reading than to try to get caught up every few months. Throw out all unread magazines once a month—if you didn't get to it by the time the next issue arrives, you won't get to it. If you don't have an office with a door you can close, find some other space that is far away from walk-in traffic.

Meet Regularly with SPOC

When I was at Bell Labs, each system administrator served two to three groups of customers (we all supported the entire network, but each SA was supposed to focus on a particular customer segment). We were required to meet with the Single Point of Contact (SPOC) for each group, along with the department head (the person who paid the bills for that group).

It was difficult to get on the department heads' schedules, but they gave in when they were promised the meeting would be kept to 15 minutes and would always start on time.

The department heads found that it was revolutionary to actually be able to communicate their needs directly to the IT staff rather than playing cat-and-mouse games. They would often ask to extend the meeting beyond 15 minutes, or they would use the first 15 minutes to set goals, and the system administrator and SPOC would continue the meeting to work on the issues raised.

Some department heads resisted, saying that they delegated "all that kind of thing" to their SPOC. However, we found that without the person who paid the bills in the room, the meetings were not as effective. Eventually, we were successful at having regular meetings with every customer group SPOC and department head because our listening skills, and later actions, demonstrated the value of the meetings.

Deleting Old Routines

Sometimes you have to update your routines.

In the "gas tank" story, earlier in this chapter, I pointed out that eventually I forgot why I had started such a routine but I continued doing it. That sounds a little dangerous. Without knowing why I was doing something, is it right to keep doing it?

I guess it comes down to faith in myself. Since I created the routine, I know I have already settled any ethical dilemmas. And I'm talking about changing backup tapes and filling gas tanks, not life-or-death decisions.

I find that routines delete themselves by becoming obsolete. When I got a promotion and someone else took responsibility for changing the backup tapes, the routine I had developed expired on its own.

Routines also modify themselves and evolve. This isn't a Perl script that, if left unmodified, will fail after the files it affects have been migrated to a new server. This is you. You're human. You see things as they happen and adjust.

Of course, I try to be flexible. When someone challenges my adherence to a particular routine, I keep an open mind and listen to his concerns. Sometimes he is even right.

Summary

- A good routine saves you work and reduces the amount of time you spend making decisions.
- Routines give you a way to "think once, do many."
- Develop the routine of always recording your appointments and to do items in your organizer and always having your organizer with you.

The more routines we develop, the less brainpower we have to put into small matters, and the more brain power we have to focus on the fun and creative parts of being a system administrator. Throughout your day, look for opportunities to create your own routines. Red flags for such opportunities include:

- Repeated events that aren't scheduled
- Maintenance tasks
- Relationships and career networking
- When procrastinating takes longer than the task
- Things you forget often
- Inconsequential or low-priority tasks that can be skipped occasionally but shouldn't be
- Developing new skills
- Keeping up-to-date

Schedule Reading Time

Never get caught up reading all those computer-industry magazines that come to your mailbox? Schedule a one-hour reading time each week. Find a place to hide, and read as much as you can. Throw out what you weren't able to read, which keeps your reading material fresh.

CHAPTER 4

The Cycle System

In 1997, I received an award for my political activism. In addition to my full-time system administration job and very active social life, I spent my spare time involved in four nonprofits, one of which I had been president of, another that I had founded. Someone asked me how I kept it all coordinated. I smiled and thanked them for the compliment, and politely held back from saying, "I'm a system administrator! I manage chaos for a living!"

The truth is that I had figured out how to keep track of the flood of requests and to do items that came my way without losing any of them. It's easy to look like you know what you're doing when you have good follow-through.

Your customers value your ability to follow through more than they value any other skill you have. Nothing ruins your reputation like agreeing to do something and forgetting to do it. The secret to perfect follow-through is to record all requests and track each request until completion. My key to perfect follow-though is a system I call *The Cycle* because it repeats every day, and the output of one day is the input to the next. Sort of like in grade-school science where you draw a circular diagram that shows how a frog starts life as an egg, becomes a tadpole, grows legs, turns into a froglet, becomes an adult frog, and gives birth to more eggs, which starts the cycle all over again. This system is just like that, except that each cycle is 24 hours, and you don't have to live in a pond.

The Cycle uses three tools: a combined to do list and today's schedule, a calendar, and a list of long-term life goals. Store all these tools in one place. The process is the same whether you use a PDA or an old-fashioned planner or organizer (PAA) that can be found in a stationery store.

Keeping all three databases in one place is important because:

- The three databases interact with each other. You want to be able to easily flip between them.

- It's easier to track the location of one thing rather than three things.
- You need to keep the databases with you all the time, and it's easier to carry a bundle than it is to carry three individual items.

This chapter explains The Cycle System in general. Chapters 5, 6, and 7 will explain The Cycle System's parts: to do lists and schedules, the calendar, and life goals. These might be the most important chapters you read in your system administration career.

USER FRIENDLY by Illiad

Don't Trust Your Brain

System administrators in general are smart people. You're smart. I'm smart. We're all smart. We've achieved our stature through brainpower, not brawn. Sure, our good looks help, but deep down ours is a "brain" job. On average, people have a short-term memory capacity of seven items, plus or minus two. What about the average reader of *this* book? I bet you're closer to eight, nine, or, heck, you in the back row reading the comic book might be as high as ten (plus or minus three).

Turning to my personal to do list, I see about 20 items. Damn. That's a lot more than 10.

There's no way I can trust my brain to remember 20 items. I need a little external storage. So do you.

I hope you aren't insulted when I say "Don't trust your brain."

I don't trust mine. That's why I write down *every request, every time.* Whether I use a PDA or PAA, when someone asks me to do something, I write it down. This has become the mantra:

Write down every request, every time.

My brain feels a little insulted by this lack of trust. When someone asks me to do something my brain starts yelling, "I'll remember it! Put down that PDA, Tom! Trust me this time!" However, all the inspiration I need to record the request is to hark back to those times when I've had to face a customer who was upset that I hadn't completed his request and deliver the rather lame excuse, "I forgot."

In Chapter 2, I discussed delegate, record, or do. When we delegate a task, we don't have to record it, though it is sometimes wise to record that we should follow up with the delegate to make sure the request was accomplished. (We are, so to speak, our brother's keeper.)

Also, if we are going to *do* the task, we don't have to write it down. If someone asks, "Please pass the salt," I don't write in my to do list, "pass the salt," and then cross it off my to do list. That would be silly. However, if someone asks me to do something and I say, "Sure, right after I'm finished with this," then I write it down. Don't confuse "when I'm finished" with doing something right away. In fact, for me, the biggest temptation to not write something down is when I think I'll remember it because it's what I'm going to be doing next.

Our poor brains. So insulted by the suggestion that they can't remember everything. However, remember that our brain is also where our ego is kept. Sometimes our ego oversteps its boundary and oversells its buddy the brain. When you hear yourself think, "I don't need to write this one down," or "I'll make an exception this time, how could I possibly forget this request?" just remember that it's your brain—ego big as Montana—overpromising like a Microsoft salesperson trying to meet his monthly quota.

> I used to think that the brain was the most wonderful organ in my body. Then I remembered who was telling me this.
>
> —Emo Philips

If it makes your brain feel less insulted, just remember that by not filling it with boring lists of to do items, we are reserving it for the powerhouse tasks. In Chapter 1, I mentioned the story about Albert Einstein trying to reserve as much of his brain as possible for physics by eliminating other brainwork, like deciding what to wear each day. Legend also has it that Einstein didn't memorize addresses or phone numbers, even his own. The important ones were written on a slip of paper in his wallet so as not to use up precious brain capacity. When someone would ask him for his own phone number he would tell them that it's in the phone book and politely ask them to look it up. Be like Einstein; reserve your brain for system administration.

If I don't have my organizer with me when someone makes a request (this usually happens when I'm on the way to the men's room), I am very forthright with putting the onus on the requester to make sure her request gets recorded. For example, I'll say, "Gosh, I'm running to a meeting and I really don't want to forget this request. Could you promise to send email to 'help' [which creates a ticket in our request tracking system] that says, 'Glenn. I need x-y-z. Ask Tom for details.'" I know that I have to put the responsibility of remembering the request on my organizer or back on the person making the request. Anything but my brain.

I don't trust my brain to remember stuff. Paper, on the other hand, I trust. Once something is written down, it's there. If I have a list of 10 to do items on a piece of paper I don't have to worry that one might vanish. Disappearing ink is something that only exists in cartoons, and a dog has never eaten my homework.

I also trust PDAs. I do fear a PDA breaking or somehow losing my data, but that's why when I do use one, it gets synced to a file server that is backed up. When compared to the number of times my brain forgets things, PDAs are nearly as reliable as paper.

The Perfect PDA Environment

When PDAs were new and models were few, I worked in an environment that standardized on a particular model. The system administration team would configure the PDA to sync to the user's home directory on the file server. Thus, the user's data was backed up regularly.

When a PDA broke, we had a spare. Slap it into the person's sync cradle and they were back in business instantly. Since everyone had the same PDA, the person would simply keep the spare while we took care of replacing the broken unit.

This was quite luxurious for the PDA users in our group. Today there is more variety in PDA hardware, which makes it more difficult to provide this service, but it can still be approximated with a little coordination.

Why Other Systems Fail

Before I reveal The Cycle System, I want to explain some systems commonly used by system administrators that don't work: The Scattered Notes System and The Ever-Growing To Do List of Doom.

The Scattered Notes System involves writing notes on random bits of paper or having multiple to do lists scattered about. My favorite is when I see a video monitor encircled with yellow rectangular sticky notes. Is each one an action item? A reminder? A phone number? Who knows? What is the priority of these? What if one falls off? There's too much chaos.

When you get assignments at a meeting, you start a new list. Now you are managing two lists. Then you lose one list because it got thrown out with other papers. Now you're missing meetings and failing to meet deadlines. Not a good situation.

The other extreme is The Ever-Growing To Do List of Doom. Usually someone realizes that having many lists or scraps of paper isn't a good way to track things, so he buys a notebook and declares that this will be his one list. No more confusion, right? He diligently carries this notebook everywhere. Any new assignments get written in the notebook, and old tasks get crossed out as they're completed. The process works great at first, but then it starts to break down. It's difficult to prioritize work. Older items get forgotten since our eyes tend to look only at the last (newest) few items.

The most important failure of this system, and why I call it a list of doom, is that it's pretty damn depressing. The list never ends. You work and work and work, and the list never seems to get any shorter! You cross off items that you complete, but new items appear at the end. The number of pages starts to accordion out as you cross off items in the middle, but there's that one item waaaaaay at the beginning that is just never going to get done. Soon you are flipping through pages of crossed-out items to find the one item that isn't crossed out. You feel stressed because you fear missing an incomplete item hidden in pages of crossed-out items.

Worst of all, this is a total self-esteem killer. You never get that big feeling of accomplishment from having completed the list because the list never gets completed. It's the List of Doom.

> Newman: I'm a United States postal worker.
>
> George: Aren't those the guys that always go crazy and come back with a gun and shoot everybody?
>
> Newman: Sometimes.
>
> Jerry: Why *is* that?
>
> Newman: Because the mail never stops. It just keeps coming and coming and coming, there's never a letup. It's relentless. Every day it piles up more and more and more! And you gotta get it out, but the more you get it out, the more it keeps coming in. And then the bar code reader breaks and it's Publisher's Clearing House day!
>
> —*Seinfeld*, episode #418, "The Old Man"

If The Scattered Notes System is too chaotic and The Ever-Growing To Do List of Doom is too depressing, then The Cycle is, as Goldilocks would say, "just right." It utilizes a device (either PDA or PAA) that you can carry everywhere with the bonus benefit of keeping everything in one place. The Cycle gives you a feeling of completion and accomplishment at the end of each day when you complete the day's list.

Systems That Succeed

I've explained why follow-through is important, that we shouldn't trust our brains, and the qualities of systems that fail. Now I'll explain what makes a system that will succeed.

A good system has the following qualities:

- **Portable.** You can take it everywhere.
- **Reliable.** It remembers everything you need, so you don't have to.
- **Manageable chunks.** Not a million little notes, not one List of Doom.

The elements we need to make a good system are:

- **Calendar.** A place to record recurring meetings, appointments, holidays, and so on.
- **Life-goals list.** A few blank pages to keep our long term goals and other notes.
- **A day-by-day section.** For each day we have:
  - **To do list.** A prioritized list *just for that day*.
  - **Schedule.** An hour-by-hour schedule for that day.

The essence of the system is the day-by-day page, which should be big enough for both that day's schedule and that day's to do list. FranklinCovey and Filofax sell stationery like that (see Figure 4-1). Alternatively, you can keep this information in a PDA. We're going to take our organizer with us everywhere we go so that if someone asks us to do something, we can record it right away and not be tempted to scribble it on a slip of paper that will be lost before we can copy it into our PAA/PDA.

The Cycle

The Cycle is the evolution of a system that has worked for me for over 10 years. It's relatively lightweight, yet it includes all the pieces a system administrator needs.

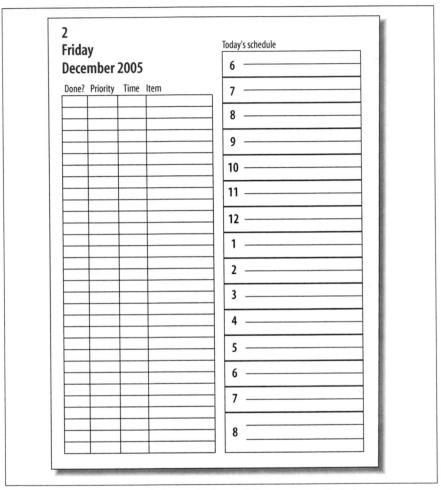

Figure 4-1. FranklinCovey, Filofax, and others sell "one page per day" sheets where you record your to do list and daily time schedule

There are four parts in our organizer:

- **365 to do lists per year.** We're going to have one to do list for each day of the year. Today's to do list records the tasks you need to do today. If you know something needs to be done on a particular day, write it on that to do list. Items left over at the end of the day will be moved to the next day's list. (If you use a PAA, you'll only need to keep the next month's worth of sheets with you. Otherwise, it will be difficult to carry!)
- **Today's schedule.** Each day we'll plan our day in one-hour increments.

- **An appointment calendar.** This will be used to record all of our appointments, meetings, social plans, and so on. Events that are further in the future than the current month are written on the calendar until they can be transferred to a particular day's schedule.

- **Notes.** Our organizer will also be used to store other notes and lists. For example, in Chapter 7, we'll create lists of short- and long-term plans.

The Cycle goes like this: each day starts by investing 10 minutes to plan my day. The planning process is simple:

- **Create today's schedule.** On today's schedule I block out time for all my meetings and appointments. All these events should already be listed on my calendar (I cover how this happens in Chapter 6). I count how many hours are remaining. Those are my work hours for the day.

- **Create today's to do list.** On today's to do list, I have a list of all the to do items I have on my plate for that day. These to do items are culled from phone calls, meetings, my calendar, our request-tracking system, and the previous day's to do list.

- **Prioritize and reschedule.** For each item, I estimate how much time the item will take to accomplish. I total the time estimates. If the total time is more than my total work hours, I move individual items to the next day's list. We'll talk about techniques for selecting what to move later.

- **Work the plan.** I spend the day working on the tasks in my list and attending meetings/appointments. I stay focused. When something is complete, I mark it with an X.

- **Finish the day.** At the end of the day, I move all the unfinished tasks to the next day's list. I mark the items that were moved with a hyphen.

- **Leave the office.** Now I can leave the office. I am happy with the knowledge that every item on my list was managed—it was either done or moved to the next day. Nothing was forgotten.

- **Repeat.** The next day The Cycle starts over again. Each day's to do list comes prepopulated with items moved from previous days.

By having a new list each day, we will get that good feeling of accomplishment when we have managed every item on today's list. When we finish our list early, we can reward ourselves by working on a "fun" project, or go home early if we have that kind of flexibility. When we have more work than can be completed today, we can feel good that we have a way to manage overflow.

We can do long- and medium-term planning instead of the constant scramble to keep our heads above water. We can break a task into smaller parts and schedule each part for a particular day. We can schedule time across the next month, or even year, to achieve a long-term goal by writing down reminders on various pages.

We also have a calendar to keep all of our appointments. Use one calendar for both work and social life because one calendar is easier to track than two. A combined calendar ensures that we don't miss something fun because we didn't check our social calendar and decided to work late.

Sound too mechanical? Too inflexible? You'll see how flexible it can be. This entire planning process will take about 10 minutes each day and save you hours of frustration. Does planning your entire day sound unrealistic? What about when new tasks are added to your to do list throughout the day? I promise we'll cover that in Chapter 5. You have to learn to crawl before you can learn to walk.

Summary

- Follow-through is the ability to make sure all requests are captured and then managed to completion (or rejection). Customers (the people you serve) and managers (the people who determine your next pay raise) value follow-through because they want to see their requests and projects completed, not dropped.
- Good follow-through is the key to good raises and promotions.
- Don't let requests become stillborn—capture all of them. When a customer sees you in the hall and requests something, don't trust your memory. If you can't write the request down, ask the customer to send the request via email or the request-tracking software. That way the onus is on the customer to make sure you don't forget his request.
- Nothing insults, infuriates, or frustrates a customer more than giving a system administrator a request and having it be forgotten.
- The more tasks you have, the harder it is to track them. Soon you are spending more time tracking the tasks than doing them.
- To remember requests, record them in a reliable way. The human brain is not as reliable as paper or electronic devices. Record requests the moment you receive them. Write down every request, every time. Reserve your brain for more important tasks.

- To do list systems fail for many reasons. Scattered notes get lost. A single list becomes a depressing Ever-Growing To Do List of Doom. These can kill self-esteem.

- The Cycle System uses a calendar for meetings, dates, and appointments; a life-goal list for long-term plans; a to do list for today (and every day); and a schedule for today that lets you plan your work.

- Every day begins by investing 10 minutes to plan your day. Examine your calendar to see how much time you have for meetings and appointments. You will use the remainder of your time for your to do list. You determine whether you have enough time to do what's on your to do list and manage any overflow. You manage the overflow by moving low-priority items to future days or renegotiating with customers.

Get Started Now!

When you begin using The Cycle it will seem awkward and difficult. However, as time goes on, it will become more comfortable. You will customize it as you start to see how it can best fit into your lifestyle. Psychologists say it takes 21 days to form a new habit; 21 days of doing the same thing over and over to make your brain treat it like a habit that can be done effortlessly. However, Tom's "one-day rule" is that you'll never get to day 21 if you don't get started. So plan on doing your new habit for one day, and make that day today. The other 20 will be a lot easier.

CHAPTER 5

The Cycle System: To Do Lists and Schedules

Now that I've teased you with an overview of The Cycle System in Chapter 4, we continue with a sequence of three chapters that explore the elements from the most immediate concern to the most long-term elements. This chapter is concerned with managing our to do list, the "now." The next chapter will discuss calendars, which are how we manage the coming days and months. Finally, we will examine long-term goal-setting in Chapter 7. Since The Cycle is a loop, there may be times when I'll gloss over a point that doesn't make sense until the other chapters have been read. You may want to cycle over these three chapters more than once.

All system administrators have one thing in common: we have too much to do and not enough hours in the day to do it. Luckily, much of this chapter deals with managing overflow. Beginning with a sample day, and then another and another, let's watch how the system works.

USER FRIENDLY by J.D. "Illiad" Frazer

A Sample Day

Let's work through a single-day example to see how the system works.

When you enter the office each morning, you should immediately focus and start this process. Otherwise, you will be caught by the interruptions and distractions that surround you: your voice mail light is flashing, people are stopping by, the coffee machine is calling you, and you are curious what *Dilbert* and the group at *User Friendly* are doing today. You decide to check your email and...hours later realize you've wasted half your day.

So **STOP**. Don't check your email or read the news sites. Instead, close your door (if you are lucky enough to have one) and follow the steps of The Cycle.

Take the Time to Plan First

"Can't I check my email first?"

No. Planning your day takes 10 minutes. Email can wait.

"What if there is an emergency and someone emailed me about it?"

Small emergencies can wait 10 minutes. Big emergencies are usually signaled by nonemail notifications, such as smoke and fire or people standing outside your door.

Here's a compromise—bring up the "dashboard" view of your network monitoring software. If it says there aren't any services down, then you don't need to check your email. (Shouldn't your monitoring software have paged you already?)

Friends tell me that they have the self-control to open up their email reader, look for important messages, and then turn it off. I don't have such self-control. I've tried checking for important messages only, but I always end up reading all my email, which leads to starting projects, and suddenly I realize I never planned my day. Trust me, the emergencies can wait 10 minutes.

Step 1: Create Today's Schedule

You begin the day by setting up today's schedule. You're going to look at your calendar to see what meetings and appointments you've committed to and use that as the basis to mark out blocks of time on your daily schedule. The remaining time can be used to work on your to do list. You'll use the power of arithmetic to calculate how much time you have.

Let's pretend you look at your calendar and see the items in Figure 5-1.

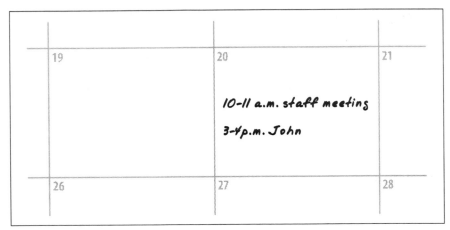

Figure 5-1. Calendar appointments

It looks like you have one-hour meetings at 10:00 a.m. and at 3:00 p.m. Therefore, you block out those times on today's schedule. You also like lunch, so you block out noon to 1 p.m. Next, you calculate how much time you have left for your to do list. It is 8:30 a.m., and you want to leave at 5:30 p.m., or in about nine hours. With three hours already blocked out, you are left with six hours to allocate to your remaining tasks. Figure 5-2 shows you what the day already looks like.

Step 2: Create Today's To Do List

Now you create the list of to do items that are on your plate for today and calculate how much work (in hours) you have. Normally, you'd have some items already scheduled. You'll add any others that come to mind (that brilliant idea you had while walking through the parking lot), and if this is the first day of the month, you'll process your life-goals list (more about that in Chapter 7).

Since this is the first day you're using The Cycle, your to do list is blank. However, you can add some items that you know you have to do. Write them in your own shorthand, not full sentences. When you write it into the to do list, it looks like Figure 5-3.

As you can see, the shorthand only has to be enough for you to understand the task. You can record as many other details, such as phone numbers, usernames, etc., as you think are necessary, but try to keep it succinct.

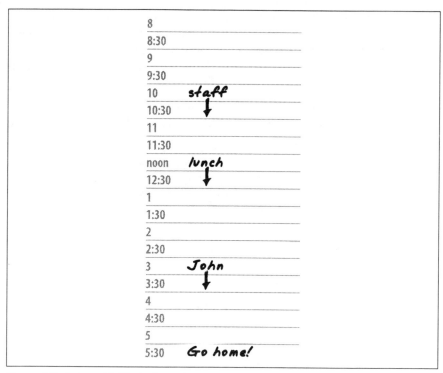

8	
8:30	
9	
9:30	
10	*staff*
10:30	↓
11	
11:30	
noon	*lunch*
12:30	↓
1	
1:30	
2	
2:30	
3	*John*
3:30	↓
4	
4:30	
5	
5:30	*Go home!*

Figure 5-2. A day with blocked-out time

Shorthand	What we know it means
Create bob smith, bsmith 555-4321	Create an account for new user Bob Smith, record his phone number (555-4321) in the account information field. We might record other details here so we don't forget them.
GCC upgrade	Install new GCC software package
Netscan off-by-1	File a bug report with the developers about the off-by-one error you found in Netscan
IDS demo	Call salesperson about scheduling a demo of a new IDS system
Bob PC	Install new PC for Bob
Tape library	Install new tape library for the new backup system
Investigation mon s'ware	Investigate new monitoring software to replace the system we're using now

Figure 5-3. Monday—to do items in your organizer

If you have voice mail waiting, this is a good time to listen to it and transcribe any messages. I tend to write down an item for each message that I get, even if the message requires no action on my part. In that case, I can mark the item as "done" right then and there. It gives me a feeling of accomplishment.

How much work do you have today? Use a column in the to do list to write an estimate of the time each item will take (Figure 5-4), and then total the estimates.

Done?	Priority	Time	Item
		15	Create bob smith, bsmith 555-4321
		2h	GCC upgrade
		30	Netscan off-by-1
		15	IDS demo
		3h	Bob PC
		2h	Tape library
		1h	Investigation mon s'ware

Figure 5-4. Monday—time estimates added

In this example, you can count the hours items (marked with an "h") quickly to see there are eight, and then total up the fractional parts (unlabeled times are in minutes) and find that they total one hour. Therefore, the amount of work on your to do list totals nine hours.

Step 3: Prioritize and Reschedule

Next, you mark each item based on a simple priority system. I tried a priority system in which I ranked items from 1 to 100, and it was too complicated. A friend pointed out that there are really three priorities in life:

- The deadline is today, and it really needs to be done now.
- The deadline is soon.
- Everything else

For the sake of simplicity, let's call these A, B, and C tasks, and that's how you will mark the tasks on your priority list. Figure 5-5 shows you how I have prioritized tasks for this first day.

Done?	Priority	Time	Item
	A	15	Create bob smith, bsmith 555-4371
	B	2h	GCC upgrade
	A	30	Netscan off-by-1
	A	15	IDS demo
	A	3h	Bob PC
	A	2h	Tape library
	C	1h	Investigation mon s'ware

Figure 5-5. Monday—priorities added

Dealing with overflow

You have nine hours of tasks on your to do list, but only six hours of time to spend working on them. How can you handle the overflow?

The wrong thing to do is to stay late. Your social life is valuable. You don't do your employer any favors by ignoring social time and becoming irritable. You work better when you eat right, get plenty of sleep regularly, exercise, and participate in nonwork activities.

The easiest thing to do is to shift the C priorities and enough of the B priorities to the next day. That's one of the benefits of having one to do list assigned to each day. We can move items around. Here are some ideas that work well:

- **Move lowest-priority tasks to the next day.** This is the most common choice for me. The reason you set priorities is because everything can't be done at once. Therefore, you take a few of the C and B priorities and move them to tomorrow.

- **Bite off today's chunk.** Bite off a more manageable portion of the task and move the rest to tomorrow. For example, installing the new tape backup system involves many, many steps. Today you can unpack it and make sure all the parts are there and that the cables will reach. Tomorrow you can recruit a volunteer to help lift the system into the rack and install it. The next day you can configure the drivers. You are fine as long as you are making progress and completing all the tasks by your deadline. Once you have broken a task into multiple parts, write each part on a different day's to do list. This is a good method for tasks that are a high risk for being stalled by unexpected roadblocks. For example, you want to do the first bite-sized chunk right away because, in doing so, you will discover any missing parts that might take a while to replace. You want to learn that a cable is missing now, not the day of the deadline.

- **Shorten the task (reduce the scope of the task).** Sometimes you can find ways to make a task take less time. For example, when installing Bob's PC, you might realize that Bob is a chatty person and the task will take half as long if you do the installation without him standing there. Alternatively, maybe you were going to put a number of extra software packages on his machine. However, Bob is fairly technical and you know that if you don't install some of the extras, he is capable of installing them himself. In fact, maybe he'll appreciate being allowed to do things his way. If he needs the additional packages, he will ask for them, or you can tell him what you didn't install and offer to come back later to install them. Now Bob gets the instant gratification of using his PC, and you can move on to other tasks. Of course, you'll write "Finish installing Bob's software" on your to do list for tomorrow so you don't forget.

- **Change the time estimate.** You should always overestimate how long something will take. It's just safer that way. However, sometimes you may go too far, and you will find you can reduce your time estimate to make things fit while still being realistic about the time commitment.

- **Delegate.** Sometimes you can find someone else to take on a task. Junior SAs look forward to being given more challenging assignments that let them learn new skills. Of course, you don't always have the authority to delegate, which brings us to the next suggestion.

- **Ask your boss for help prioritizing.** When you have a full to do list, prioritized and annotated with realistic time estimates, you can really wow your boss by showing the list to her and asking for help setting priorities. If you've never done this, it might sound like I'm describing some kind of fantasy land, but the truth is that managers often feel like they have very little power over what their staff does, and it is quite a breath of fresh air to be asked, "Am I prioritizing these correctly?" (Of course, if you do this every day you'll get dinged on the "works independently" question on your yearly evaluation.) Once when I did this, my boss was able to clarify the priorities he wanted me to work on, which helped me in general. Another time, my boss saw a few to do items that he hadn't realized the team was involved with and eliminated them (his words were, "Joe Schmoe needs to learn to do that himself. I'm going to have a talk with his manager"). Sometimes I've had entire categories of tasks removed ("Tell Joe we no longer support that, and if he has a problem he should talk with me"), and occasionally my boss has delegated tasks to other coworkers. I find most SAs don't know that this option exists and yet, used judiciously, it can be the most powerful time management tool around.

- **Delay a meeting or appointment.** Delaying a meeting can be really bad. Rescheduling can be a nightmare, or annoy many people, or possibly delay a project. However, you can voluntarily miss a meeting or send a delegate. If you are supposed to attend a two-hour meeting—just to make sure that when the new server is discussed you can point out that it only comes in blue, not red—send a delegate to do that. (And if it starts a major discussion, the delegate can call you into the meeting.) Postponing an appointment is better than missing an appointment. I've found that when I postpone an appointment in person or via phone (i.e., not via email, which is not very interactive) often the person is able to shorten the appointment (cut to the chase). Oh, all he really wanted was to know whether the server was going to be red or blue? Well, it's going to be blue.

- **Work late.** I'm listing this option purely for completeness. This has got to be the worst option. Most people have four to five productive hours in them each day. Anything more is spinning your wheels. That's why books like *Extreme Programming* (O'Reilly) and *PeopleWare* (Dorset House) recommend eliminating overtime. However, it's also part of the SA's job to work late sometimes. As we discussed in the section "Delegate, Record, or Do" in Chapter 2, when there is an emergency, customers expect all hands to be working on the issue until it is resolved.

Back to our example to do list:

Let's *move low-priority tasks to the next day*. You have one C priority called "Investigate mon s'ware." Let's move this to the next day.

If you are using a PDA, you bump the entry to the next day's list. If you are using a PAA, mark the entry with a hyphen to indicate that it was moved, and hand copy the entry to the next day's to do list.

You've reduced today's workload by one hour. You still need to eliminate two more hours.

Luckily, you also have a B priority (GCC upgrade) that can be moved to the next day. You move it the same way as you did the C priorities (PDA: bump it; PAA: mark it with a hyphen in today's list and handwrite it into tomorrow's list). Now your list looks like Figure 5-6 and matches your number of available hours.

Done?	Priority	Time	Item
	A	15	Create bob smith, bsmith 555-4321
—	B	2h	GCC upgrade
	A	30	Netscan off-by-1
	A	15	IDS demo
	A	3h	Bob PC
	A	2h	Tape library
—	C	1h	Investigation mon s'ware

Figure 5-6. A fully loaded Monday with overflow priorities moved to Tuesday

Dealing with Long-Term Projects

How do you deal with a long term-project? When a to do item is going to take six months, how do you work that into the time estimates for today?

It is important to break big projects into smaller steps or milestones. Very big projects often have project managers who do that for you. For your own projects, you need to do this for yourself. Take a moment to break the project into parts and estimate how long each will take. Write each milestone on the to do list of the day you are supposed to start working on it, or mark it on your calendar if it is far enough out. It's this kind of planning that really impresses managers.

On my daily to do list, I write the name of the project and the current milestone. That way I'm reminded of the larger goal as I work on each daily task. For example, I might write "Network Reorg—map current network."

Step 4: Work the Plan

Spend the day working as close to the plan as possible. First do the A items, then the B items, and then, if you have time, the C items.

It can be useful to have some kind of alarm or reminder to tell you when your meetings and appointments are so that you don't have to keep interrupting yourself to look at the clock.

When you finish one task, start on the next task. Keep the momentum going.

Many people have told me that they spend a lot of time trying to decide what to do next. A simple solution is to do all the A priorities in the order they appear on the list, and then do the same with the Bs and the Cs. We'll improve upon that system in Chapter 8, but for now, you can't do too badly by just doing them in order. The items higher on the page tend to be things that were copied from previous days. In other words, items you've put off tend to bubble up to the top of the list and will get taken care of first.

Try to take advantage of your momentum by moving onto the next task after you complete a task. Do this even if a task took less time than you had planned; it will make up for time lost when another task takes longer than expected.

Once in a while, pause to stretch. If you finish a task early, take a quick walk around the building. Being in IT generally means you don't get enough exercise. Carry a file folder so it looks like you are on your way to something important—nobody will be the wiser.

Once you've finished all your As, start working on the Bs. If you finish those, congratulate yourself by working on the most fun C item on the list.

Step 5: Finish the Day

It's rare that you will complete everything on your to do list, but you do want to make sure that the items are all managed. An item is *managed* if you've given it sufficient attention on that day.

A half-hour before the end of your day, look at the remaining items. If there are any As that aren't complete, you need to manage that situation. Call the person expecting the task to be completed and come up with a contingency plan. Or, if these are self-imposed deadlines (and they often are), copy the items to the next day.

In our example, you had enough time to unpack your tape library, make sure it came with the right cables, and even pantomime the process of mounting it in the rack to make sure the cables would reach and so on. However, you weren't able to find anyone to help you lift it into the rack. Therefore, you managed the item by noting what you did accomplish (checking off the items) and copying the remaining parts of the project to the next day.

With a PDA, you would bump the item to Tuesday's list. With a PAA, you can write in "unpacked and checked" next to the item, mark it with a hyphen, and write "mount tape library" on Tuesday's list.

Any remaining Bs and Cs should also be moved to the next day. In our example, there aren't any to be moved because we moved them already. Our lists now look like Figure 5-7. As you can see, it took us six hours to complete five hours of tasks.

Done?	Priority	Time	Item
✗	A	15	~~Create bob smith, bsmith 555-4321~~
—	B	2h	GCC upgrade
✗	A	30	~~Netscan off-by-1~~
✗	A	15	~~IDS demo~~
✗	A	3h	~~Bob PC~~
—	A	2h	Tape library unpacked & checked
—	C	1h	Investigation mon s'ware

Figure 5-7. Monday's to do list at the end of the day

Step 6: Leave the Office

Figure 5-7 shows a list on which every item in the Done? column has a mark. You've managed every item on your list. No, they aren't all completed, but they were managed. Sometimes managing an item means making sure it got the appropriate amount of attention; for low-priority items, that means they were moved to tomorrow. The important thing is that they were not forgotten.

You can look at your to do list and get the satisfaction of knowing you've managed everything on your plate today. Congratulate yourself. Smile. Put your coat on and go home happy. You deserve it.

I used to leave work every day feeling terrible. I felt like I had worked and worked, but I felt no sense of accomplishment. When I use The Cycle, I'm able to look at my list of items, see that each one was managed, and feel closure. I can leave the office with a smile on my face.

Step 7: Repeat

Let's pretend it's Tuesday. You can repeat The Cycle with today's list of items.

Today I'll introduce some advanced topics and show you how to manage them. In particular, you'll see how The Cycle works with a request-tracking system, voice mail messages, and interruptions.

Create today's schedule

You should start each day by checking your calendar for any appointments and filling them into your day's schedule. Today you have no meetings, so your hour-by-hour schedule is blank except for one hour for lunch, which leaves you eight hours for work out of your typical nine-hour day.

So far, so good!

Create today's (Tuesday's) to do list

Yesterday, four new tasks were added to your plate. Let's call them Task1, Task2, Task3, and Task4. They're low-priority tasks delegated to you during the staff meeting. They were not as important as the tasks you had to do yesterday, so you recorded them directly onto the first to do list that you thought was realistic, which happened to be today's (Tuesday's). This is in addition to the tasks that you managed yesterday by placing them on today's to do list.

When you arrived at your office today, your voice mail light was flashing, so you listened to the three messages and recorded them in your to do list, even if they didn't require any action.

It turns out that the first one was a company-wide notice about the east entrance of your building being blocked. You're *so glad* they're wasting time for everyone in the company because obviously you would *never* have realized what all the construction equipment and the big freakin' signs that say *East Exit Closed* could possibly have meant. Since this doesn't require any action from you, you promptly cross the item out.

The next message is from your Cisco salesperson. You record the number, since you're going to call him back (but before you cross out the item, you will verify that your contact database—described in Chapter 12—has the same number listed). The third message is a salesperson cold-calling you. You're not going to return that call, so you just write "junk" and mark an X in the Done? column. Your Tuesday list now looks like Figure 5-8.

The day hasn't started, and you've already completed two items! You rule!

You might be wondering why you write down a task that you immediately mark as completed. You do this because it becomes a log of your phone calls, which can be a good "cover your ass" measure. This is one reason I prefer a PAA to a PDA. With a PAA, it's less effort to write junk items that immediately get crossed off.

Done?	Priority	Time	Item
		1h	*Investigation mon s'ware*
		2h	*GCC upgrade*
		1h	*Mount tape library*
		1h	*Task 1*
		1h	*Task 2*
		1h	*Task 3*
		1h	*Task 4*
✗			~~*vm: East exit blocked*~~
		1s	*vm: Cisco, Joe +1 800-555-1111*
✗			~~*vm: junk*~~

Figure 5-8. Tuesday—after listening to your voice mail

I've already mentioned a couple of times that having some kind of request-tracking system is a good idea. How do you handle that in The Cycle System? You designate a specific amount of time each day to work on your tickets. I once had a job where I was expected to spend one-third of my day working on such requests. Therefore, every day I added a two-hour task called Tickets to my list. I wouldn't handle those tickets only during a two-hour block in the morning, but rather I used Tickets as a time holder for those moments in the day when I needed to work on tickets because one of them had become an unexpected priority.

I also get a lot of interruptions, about one hour's worth a day. These interruptions are an important part of serving my customers' needs, so I also allocate time for them.

 If I've set up a mutual interruption shield, I write "MIS" for the time I'm the shield. Any project work I get done during that time is a bonus.

Now you can calculate how many hours of work you have to do, and it turns out to be 11.25 hours! With only 8 hours to do 11.25 hours of work, it's time to prioritize. Any "due today" items immediately become an A priority. The tape library issue was an A yesterday, which we half-completed. Therefore, finishing that task is obviously an A priority today.

Prioritize and reschedule

How do you prioritize the Tickets and Interruptions items? Well, they have to be done every day, so they should be As. However, Interruptions is sort of a buffer just in case you are interrupted, so you can be flexible and mark that item as a B.

There are a few Bs and lots of Cs (which is normal). Thus, you have something that looks like Figure 5-9.

Done?	Priority	Time	Item
	C	1h	*Investigation mon s'ware*
	B	2h	*GCC upgrade*
	A	1h	*Mount tape, library*
	C	1h	*Task 1*
	C	1h	*Task 2*
	C	1h	*Task 3*
	C	1h	*Task 4*
X			~~*vm: East exit blocked*~~
	A	1s	*vm: Cisco, Joe +1 800-555-1111*
X			~~*vm: junk*~~
	A	2h	*Tickets*
	B	1h	*Interruptions*

Figure 5-9. Tuesday's tasks after filling in all time estimates and priorities

Yesterday, the sum of the As and Bs was more hours than could fit into your day, so you had to use our techniques to shift work to the next day. Today, the sum of the As and Bs is only 6.25 hours. Because that will fit in your eight-hour day, there isn't any overflow that we have to move.

I've found that if I only have a few As and complete them early in the day, the rest of the day is more relaxed. I do my Bs and as many of the other tasks as possible, and when the end of the day comes, I move the incomplete work to the next day without guilt. It's a lot less stressful this way, and it allows me to deal with interruptions a lot better. Let's use that technique today.

You won't slide any tasks onto Wednesday's to do list right now. As you'll see, you'll do that at the end of the day, if necessary.

Work the plan

Now you work on the As until they are complete. Working on tickets might generate more action items for you. For example, if a request is not going to be completed in one sitting, you can add it to your to do list. Let's say ticket #43001 from RT involves fixing a nightly batch job and then verifying that the fix worked. You can fix the problem, then create a to do item on the next day to verify that the change fixed the problem (Figure 5-10).

Done?	Priority	Time	Item
		15	43001: check batch

Figure 5-10. Adding a request-tracking ticket to Wednesday

If another ticket involves ordering software and installing it, you might order the software today and then write an item for the day that you expect it to arrive.

I use my organizer to track any ticket that I'm actively working on. The list of tickets that I own, however, is much longer; therefore, I don't include them in my personal to do list. I use my to do list only to track the things I'm actively working on and things that I need to do on a specific date in the future.

PDA Integration for Request-Tracking Software

I have not seen request-tracking software that integrates with PDAs. I'm sure it exists, I just haven't seen it yet.

If a request-tracking system were integrated into PDA software, I might track tickets I was actively working on as As or Bs, and all on-hold tickets would be tracked as Zs. I could imagine that when a ticket grows closer to its deadline, the system would automatically promote it to an A priority. The key feature of such a system would be to insert tickets into my to do list but not require everything in my list to be a ticket. If I include "pick up laundry" in my to do list, I don't want the system to enter that into the corporate database.

Next, you work on the Bs. Since Interruptions is a buffer, you don't have to stand around doing nothing if nobody interrupts you.

Finish the day and leave the office

At the end of the day, you spend a few minutes managing the remaining items. The tasks that haven't been completed are moved to the next day, and you leave the office with a smile on your face knowing that you've managed all of your tasks.

Other Tips

The system is flexible enough that as you face new situations, you can adapt the system to handle them. This section lists some of the techniques I've found useful.

Large Projects

When dealing with a large project, split it into individual steps and sprinkle the tasks across to do lists on different days. For example, write a step on each Monday during the month that the task must be completed.

What to Do When You Finish Early

What should you do when a miracle happens and you run out of things to do? I think you should reward yourself. Here are some good reward ideas:

- Get a head start on tomorrow's tasks.
- Dig deep into that pile of dream projects that you've always wanted to do.
- Read from that stack of magazines that's been accumulating.
- Go through your request tracker and clean up old tickets.
- Clean your office, your email inbox, your computer room, or lab.
- Visit your boss's office and ask for more work. (Just kidding!)
- Sit in your office for 15 minutes doing nothing. Trouble will find you.
- If you have a flexible work environment, why not take the rest of the day off? You deserve it!

New Tasks Given to You During the Day

Let's suppose you've planned the perfect day. You have calculated each task down to the minute, and you know you'll be done and ready to leave right at the end of the day.

Of course, thinking like this is asking for trouble. It's days like this that your boss comes into your office around 2 p.m. with a "brilliant" idea that includes many multihour tasks, thereby disrupting your perfect plan.

That is, of course, why I only recommend planning rough estimates of how long tasks will take.

So, what do you do when new tasks are thrown at you all day long? We've already seen the technique of scheduling one hour per day for interruptions, but when a much longer project interrupts (say, a three-hour outage), we must reshuffle.

Calculate how much time you have left in the day and see whether your A and B priorities will fit into that time. If not, use the techniques to shift them to the next day. Usually all the Bs and Cs get shifted. If there isn't enough time for your A priorities, you need to talk with the person expecting those tasks to be completed. It may be your boss, who will hopefully understand and help you reprioritize your tasks. However, it may be someone else, and he deserves at least an email explaining that there was an emergency and that his request will be completed tomorrow.

Personal Tasks

I use the same to do list system for managing my personal to do tasks. Everything from laundry to shopping items goes in my organizer. That way, I get more practice at using the system, which benefits me at work.

If I used a different system for work and nonwork activities, I would have to carry around two different organizers—carrying one is enough!

Since I use a PAA, I can position items on the page. That is, I write my personal items toward the bottom of each day's to do sheet. That breaks it into two different lists on the same page. If you use a PDA, there may be another trick you can perform, such as assigning the task to a category.

When I leave work, I always check my nonwork items to see whether there is anything I need to do on the way home.

Setting Up a PAA for Use with The Cycle

If you use a PAA (paper notebook), you can find filler paper that fits all of the following needs at a stationery store. You will need:

- 12 full-page calendars (one for each month).

- Enough note paper for each day of the year. Stationery stores have such paper preprinted with the dates January 1 through December 31. It usually has room for today's schedule on one side and today's to do list on the other. All you need to do is load the next 30 days once a month.
- Extra note pages kept in the back for keeping your list of life goals, other lists, and notes as you see fit (optional).
- A binder or notebook to keep it all together.

If your projects are small, you might be able to make due with a small datebook. Larger ones contain at least a few lines per day to keep notes. However, you might not be able to keep many to do items in such a book.

Setting Up a PDA for Use with The Cycle

If you use a PDA, you have many choices. PDAs usually come with software that lets you keep an appointment calendar, to do lists, and notes. However, there is a wealth of aftermarket add-on packages that can greatly enhance the experience.

DateBook (DB) V (*http://www.pimlicosoftware.com*) won my favor early on because it makes implementing the "to do list per day" concept very easy. I like to think of it as finishing what Palm set out to do. A Palm-based PDA without DateBook V is a toy. DB V makes to do entry very fast through the use of templates, uses color effectively to highlight what's important, and can give advanced warning of an event. This last feature is particularly useful to me. Before DB V, I had to enter a reminder for someone's birthday and plug in an additional reminder a week early so that I had time to buy a gift. With DB V, I can simply request advance warning of an anniversary or birthday. DB V is only available for PalmOS. One of the nice things about DB is that it maintains its data in the normal PalmOS data structures, so all your items sync just as you would hope they do.

Life Balance (LB) (*http://www.llamagraphics.com*) is not just great software, it's a great philosophy. LB has all the important features of The Cycle (to do lists, calendars, and so on), but it adds the important concept of being aware that your life needs balance. Maybe you've decided you want to split your time between three projects plus home life. If you've been ignoring one of those categories, to do items from that area will start appearing higher in your priority list. Eventually your life is back in balance. It's a great concept and many people swear by this software. It's available for Mac OS X and Windows, and it syncs to a PalmOS version.

Once, while I was teaching my Time Management for System Administrators seminar, someone said that when he's done with one task, he wishes someone else would pick the next task for him. He said he spends too much time worrying about what to do next. That's when someone else chimed in about Life Balance. You program it with how you want your life balanced, and it sees to it that you meet those goals.

Another nice thing about Life Balance is that rather than putting each to do item in a category such as Work or Home, you mark each item with the location(s) in which you are able to do that task. So, the next time you are at the grocery store (or your boss's office), you click on that place, and Life Balance shows a list of things that need to be done there. Very convenient!

What do I use? I've tried a variety of platforms. However, I must admit that I always returned to the first platform I learned: a leather-bound binder with preprinted paper filler for each day of the year. I think that if the first platform I used had been a peanut butter and banana sandwich, I would always return to it, because once I develop a habit, I tend to stick with it.

In all other aspects of my life, I'm fairly high-tech and upgrade to new systems regularly. I switch computers and operating systems constantly. I used email long before it was a household word, I set up one of the largest WiFi networks before it was called WiFi, and I bought a Tivo before most of my friends knew it existed. However, for my time management, I like paper. I like to write in large letters, scribble, draw arrows and circles. When someone starts rattling off information to me, I like to be able to start writing it down immediately, not wait for a microprocessor to get out of sleep mode. I used the same large-size (8.5"×11") leather-bound binder from 1991 until 2004, and then switched to a smaller (5.5"×8.5") one (but still leather!) in January of 2005.

I'm just a creature of habit.

The point is that what you use is what works for you. Try them all (especially the software—they usually have a free trial download). Borrow a few PDAs from friends and coworkers, even if it is just for a few minutes during lunch. Spend time in a stationery store getting a feel for various date books and planner systems.

Take Responsibility When Vendors Don't Follow Through

Follow-through doesn't just mean tracking issues. Follow-through is about results. A coworker of mine couldn't understand why his boss was unhappy with his performance when a project was delayed because a vendor hadn't returned a call placed two weeks earlier. It wasn't his fault that the vendor hadn't called back, right?

That's not how the world works. You can't assume that a vendor will call back. You have to take responsibility for a project's timely completion. Here are some tips:

- **Call the vendor once a day until you connect.** Call every day. Don't wait for them to take the initiative.

- **Call the vendor early in the morning.** If you reach them early in the day, they can spend the rest of the day working their bureaucracy to get you the answer or result you need. If you call them at the end of the day, then your request gets forgotten by morning. (They haven't read this book.)

- **Log that you've called the vendor in your organizer.** The log may prove useful when things go really wrong.

- **Always leave voice mail.** You need to leave proof that you called. Without leaving a message, it's the same as not calling. You don't have to be original each time. Simply say, "This is [your name here]. Please call me at [your phone number]. I need [status update/whatever] about [project]. Thank you." If you don't give a reason for calling, you'll end up playing phone tag. If you say what you need, the vendor can work on it whether or not they are able to reach you. However, be brief and leave your phone number at the beginning of the message, not the end.

Related to this, the order isn't "in" until a shipper's tracking number and/or delivery date is provided.

I've been stung many times by vendors (and purchasing departments) that were late to ship something. "Oh, I'd been sitting on this order for a week because there's a form you need to fax me." Why didn't they tell me? Don't these people work on commission? Have they found some magical business model where *not* shipping a product makes them money?

—continued—

The wrong question to ask, and I know this because I used it unsuccessfully for years, is, "Do you need anything else from me?" Silly me. I thought that a highly motivated salesperson would take this opportunity to finish the deal so he could get commission. No, the real problem is that not all roadblocks involve me. Maybe a credit approval needs to be finished or a design needs to receive an internal sign-off. Technically, those involve someone from the purchasing department, not me. People don't want to feel that they are making work for you, so they are polite and answer no to this question. In reality, if I know of the roadblocks that aren't in my control, at least I can manage them—i.e., I can start calling the purchasing department to make sure they clear the roadblock.

Therefore, when it seems like everything is done, I ask the magic question: "Can you tell me what date it will arrive?" Suddenly it clicks in the salesperson's brain to tell me that I really am done or to list the roadblocks: the product isn't available until next spring, or that while I've filled out the credit application, he hasn't submitted it to his finance department. These are both real examples.

Once I get a delivery date, the question changes to, "Can you give me a tracking number?" That's the real proof that the order hasn't hit any snags. For important projects, I call every day until I receive a tracking number. I always call in the morning, and I always leave a polite message if I'm transferred to someone's voice mail.

Summary

- The day is spent working based on the plan. Mark completed items with an X and items moved to the next day with a hyphen.

- Toward the end of the day, manage any incomplete items so that the people who made the requests are not surprised to learn of the delay.

- By the end of the day, all items have been managed, meaning they have either been completed or somehow worked into future days. The point is, rather than going home feeling like you still have a huge burden, you can go home feeling that all tasks have been managed. You can go home with a smile, knowing that you did today's work. Tomorrow's work will tend to itself.

- If you finish early, reward yourself. You can do a personal project, get caught up on work-related reading, clean/organize your office, get ahead on tomorrow's tasks, and so on. If you have a flexible work environment, you can go home early.

- When new tasks are given to you during the day, you can schedule them for tomorrow or reshuffle today's plan to fit them in. If you consistently get new tasks throughout the day that have to be done "right now," you can allocate a certain amount of interruption time each day when you create your plan.

- Personal tasks can be managed using the same system. By using one system for both work and nonwork tasks, you get more practice at using The Cycle, you have only one system to carry around, and you benefit from not forgetting the nonwork stuff that makes your life better.

- The system you use isn't as important as having a system. That is, The Cycle System works for me—if you have a different system that works for you, use it. However, if you are reading this book, there is a good chance you don't have a system. Try The Cycle for a while, then start customizing it for your work habits and lifestyle.

- The Cycle can be done with either a PDA or the pen-and-paper equivalent, a PAA. Each of these has pros and cons. Try both and use the one that works for you.

## CHAPTER 6

The Cycle System: Calendar Management

Chapter 5 was the closeup look at how to plan an individual day using a to do list as part of The Cycle System introduced in Chapter 4. In this chapter, we'll see how effective calendar management keeps track of your routines and links individual days into a coherent whole.

Every organizer has a calendar section, sometimes called a datebook. The calendar is both a repository for information you need for a given day (appointments, deadlines, birthdays, milestones) and a wide-view tool for long-range planning (career advancement, long-term project completion, vacation planning).

Calendars let us see the big picture. Early in my career as a system administrator, I was constantly worried that I wasn't seeing the big picture of what I was doing. I always seemed to be working hard just to stay in one place. What turned that around for me was thinking in terms of calendars. Sure, the daily to do list helps me think about what I'm doing today, but with a big calendar, I could see the big picture.

USER FRIENDLY by Illiad

How to Use Your Calendar

The Cycle uses the calendar part of your organizer for three primary purposes. First, to block out time for events and meetings that are further in the future than today's schedule. Second, to list any reminders or milestones such as birthdays and anniversaries. Finally, if you use a PAA, the calendar is where you can record to do items that are further in the future than your current daily filler paper permits. Here are descriptions of calendar items in more detail:

- **Appointments and meetings.** Any time you agree to an appointment or meeting, record it in the calendar. Use the calendar to block out future responsibilities. This also helps you to prevent conflicts.

- **Milestones.** Record birthdays, anniversaries, and other important dates in the calendar—for example, company holidays and when coworkers are going to be on vacation.

- **Future to do items.** Finally, if you use a PAA, you can use your calendar to record to do items that are far in the future. For example, chances are that only the next month's worth of per-day to do list sheets fit in your PAA. If you have to do maintenance on a fancy color printer two months after it is installed, you can mark that to do item on your calendar two months after installation and transfer it to your daily to do list when that day arrives.

It's rather simple: always record everything, and always use your calendar to guide your day.

When you take 10 minutes to plan your day, start by reviewing what you've recorded in the calendar entry for today. It points out meetings and appointments that you've committed to; use this information to make your day's schedule. To do items noted in your calendar are transferred onto today's to do list. Milestones and deadlines may translate into additional to do items.

The calendar squares on my PAA are fairly large. I like that. It gives me enough room to use the different parts of the square for different purposes. At the very top I write in birthdays and anniversaries. Slighty lower I mark vacations and anything that will last multiple days. I use the very bottom to list my nighttime activity. Since I usually only have one such activity, I reserve the last line for that. The middle I fill in proportionally with the commitments of the day. Lunch in the center, morning appointments above, and afternoon appointments below. See Figure 6-1 for an example.

The difficult part is developing the habit of recording everything. The remaining parts of this section give tips and tricks that will help you do that.

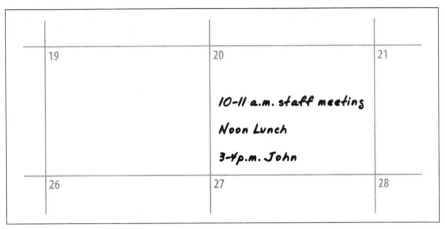

19	20	21
	10-11 a.m. staff meeting	
	Noon Lunch	
	3-4 p.m. John	
26	27	28

Figure 6-1. Sample square from my calendar

Never Miss a Meeting or Event

Are you the kind of person who misses meetings and appointments? Do you find yourself apologizing to people at work because you've agreed to meet with them about an issue, but then you didn't show up? You had an excellent reason; there was something else you were working on, and you forgot. The bad news is that "I forgot" is not a good excuse.

Nothing hurts your reputation more than being a no-show for a meeting with a customer. The first step to being seen as reliable is to always be there when you say you will be. Of course, missing the fun and/or beneficial events in life isn't good for you either.

Being on time demonstrates responsibility and projects an image of reliability to the people you work with. It shows respect for other people's meetings when you attend them on time, and then they reciprocate when they attend your meetings.

The key to never missing a meeting is this: always use your calendar. Write down all your appointments; don't commit to an appointment until you've checked your calendar for conflicts.

And, most importantly, don't rely on your brain. An organizer is the right tool for recording dates; your brain isn't. I've said this several times already, and it's only Chapter 6. You'll hear me say this again: save your brain for higher-level thinking. Use your organizer for storing information. Don't trust your brain.

I have a little confession. I used to miss appointments all the time. Worse yet, I would double-book myself. When making appointments, I'd agree to a date without checking my calendar. It was arrogant, but I would think to myself, "Hmm...June 4th. That date sounds familiar, but I can't remember anything on that date, so it must be free." Of course, the reason it was such a familiar date was because I had something scheduled then!

It was embarrassing. Calling someone to reschedule wastes time and creates work for the other person. The time I've spent fixing double bookings in my life is time I'll never get back. Luckily, that is a thing of the past for me because I'm tenacious about recording everything in my calendar.

OK, another confession. The excuse I made to myself for not checking my calendar was that I was too embarrassed to say to someone, "Please wait a moment while I get my calendar." I had an irrational fear that asking people to wait for me was a huge burden on them. Of course, it wasn't, and the hassle of asking someone to reschedule was an even bigger burden for them. I know it's silly, but I had developed a very bad habit. (Others have shared with me that they fear it will make them sound pompous and self-important: "Look at me! I'm so in-demand that I have a calendar to track all my appointments. I'll pencil you in.")

Finally, I decided that I had to break this bad habit. I remember the fear I felt the first time I asked someone to wait while I check my calendar. I made a big production out of it. "OK, that sounds good. Would you hold on while I get my calendar to make sure I'm available?" I then waited for her to respond as if I had asked her something crazy such as whether I could borrow money, or for her to name the capitol of Wisconsin. I think I broke into a sweat. Finally, she responded: yes, it was OK with her. Moments later, I returned with my calendar. She wasn't upset that I had made her wait. She understood my need to get my calendar. Heck, she did it herself. My rush-rush personality wasn't crushed by the delay. The world hadn't ended.

I hope that learning that about me will make you feel like your insecurities aren't so bad. If I can survive that, you can, too.

So, take a moment right now and start using your calendar. Pick an event and write it down (if you don't have any, make an appointment with yourself to have lunch tomorrow).

The first time you do something is always the most difficult. Maybe you've never used that part of your PDA, or you may have to run to the stationery store to buy filler paper for your PAA.

I'll wait (even if you have to run to the store).

OK, are you back? Did you record your appointment?

There, that wasn't so bad, was it?

Always Call If You Are Going to Be Late or Miss an Appointment

It is better to call someone when the meeting is supposed to be starting than to leave him wondering where you are. Even if your lateness is embarrassing, in this age of ubiquitous cell phones, there's no excuse for not calling. In an office environment, it can be useful to have a list of phone extensions in the various meeting rooms so that you can quickly get ahold of anyone.

A brief statement, such as "I'm calling because I'm going to be late," is a lot better than a rambling five-minute apology after you have already arrived late.

Of course, never lie. Telling the truth is better because then you don't have to remember who you've lied to or what lie you told. That's a lot of extra work for your brain, which we want to reserve for what's important.

One Calendar for Business and Social Life

Balance is important. Work, family life, social life, volunteer work, personal projects, sleep—these are all important things. I'm a firm believer in using one calendar for all of them.

The reason to maintain one consolidated calendar (or merged calendar view) is that it helps prevent your work life from overrunning your nonwork life. When you are about to agree to work late, you can look at your calendar and verify that you are actually free.

I used to leave work and then realize that I had a party or something fun to go to. I would drive like a maniac to get there before it ended. When I did arrive, I was too angry with myself for being late or forgetful to really enjoy the party. Now if there is something fun after work, it's part of my daily plan. Being on time for a party is as important to me as finishing a project on deadline. I give my full effort during the day, but nighttime is my time.

Most PDA software lets you keep multiple calendars but merge them into one display. In fact, it can be useful to configure your PDA synchronization software to not sync personal items onto your work PC (and work items onto your personal PC). You might not want your party plans synced to your work computer.

Automated Reminders for PAA Users

Unlike a PDA, a PAA can't be programmed to beep when it's time to leave for an appointment. What can you do instead?

Program another system to beep or alert you about the day's appointments. Make it part of your morning routine. Keep your PAA as the master calendar but program some software-based system with today's appointments.

Some good reminder systems:

- Windows and Mac users can use any of the various alarm clock programs that are out there. Search on Google for "software alarm clock," and you'll find many, ranging from free to medium priced.

- Applications like Mac iCal, Windows Outlook, and open source tools like Evolution and KOrganizer can alert you when an appointment grows near (this is useful if you are always near the machine running said software).

- Set some kind of alarm for your next appointment, either on your watch or cell phone.

- Users of Unix systems such as Mac OS X, BSD, Debian Linux, and HP Tru64 Unix have the "leave" command to alert them when to leave for an appointment.

- Program a server to send a reminder to your cell phone or pager at the appropriate time. Unix/Linux users will find it useful to enable the "at" service and use it to send email to your cell phone at a certain time:

    ```
    $ at 11:50
    > echo Meet Bob for lunch | mail 19085552323@teleflip.com
    > ^D
    ```

Remember, when setting an alarm, always set it to give yourself enough time to get to the appointment, whether that is two minutes to walk down the hall or two hours to drive to another location.

Repeating Tasks

History repeats itself. So do status and staff meetings, oil changes, El Niño, and a good burrito. A lot of the routines developed in the previous chapter become recurring events. One of the benefits of a PDA over a PAA is that recurring events can be scheduled once, and the PDA does the work of calculating all the subsequent dates.

Here are some of the things you might want to put into your calendar:

- Weekly meetings.
- Regular appointments.

- Upcoming conferences.
- Vacation plans.
- Deadlines.
- Party invites. (I record them when I RSVP. I even record them when I decline so that I don't accidentally repeat my rejection.)
- Your kid's soccer schedule.
- The date your company's quarterly report tends to come out.
- Every single birthday you ever hear mentioned. (Include celebrities! It can be fun to point out, on April 20, that today is Tito Puente's birthday.)
- Talk Like A Pirate Day (September 19), Towel Day (May 25), and System Administrator Appreciation Day (last Friday of July).

Take a moment to record those things in your PDA right now. Then develop the habit of recording any new date the moment you hear it.

We Record What We Value

Writing something in your calendar is also a demonstration that you value it. When you agree to meet a customer at a certain time and place, it shows that you value the appointment when you record it right in front of her. This is true for work-related and social appointments. Imagine if you asked someone out on a date and then, after negotiating a mutually agreeable time and place, she opens her organizer and writes down the date. Feels rather validating, doesn't it?

An instructor at a time management class told me how he discovered that his very young daughter understood that a recorded appointment is one that won't be forgotten. After agreeing to take her to the zoo the following weekend, she pulled out a big green crayon and leaned over to his PAA and wrote "ZOO!" in two-inch-tall letters. It was completely adorable.

Repeating Tasks on a PAA

If you use a PAA, there are ways to not forget recurring events. It basically comes down to being your own reminder system. I keep a weekly, monthly, and yearly list of reminders in my PAA. On every Monday, I read the weekly sheet and fill in any items for the remaining week. On the first of each month, I read the monthly sheet and fill in this month's commitments. On the first day of the year, I fill in the yearly items.

Not to put too fine a point on it, here's exactly what I do:

The bookmark I use in my PAA is a clear plastic holder for a small piece of paper. On that piece of paper I have recorded all my weekly meetings. On Monday I mark my weekly meetings on the schedules for every day this week. If I'm having a light week, I just use the list on my bookmark for reference each day.

The monthly commitments are processed when I load the next 30 days' worth of sheet-per-day filler into my PAA. That can be any time of the month. Though, for monthly meetings, it can be better to just mark the calendar for the remainder of the year. One nonprofit I work with publishes a list of all its meetings for the next year every December. When I receive that sheet, I just mark all the meetings in my calendar right then and there.

The yearly commitments are mostly birthdays and such. Those I keep in a list on my computer. (I lied earlier. It made the sentence structure more readable.) When I buy new filler paper each year, I use that list to mark these dates. My tradition is to spend time on New Year's Day every year copying the yearly dates into their space on my calendar.

A PDA can also record dates far in the future, such as conferences, etc. The filler paper I buy for my PAA comes with a sheet for listing dates in future years. When I change paper each year, I refer to those pages and fill in the appropriate calendar spaces for this year. I have been able to reschedule conflicts for graduations and weddings two and three years in advance.

Know Your Personal Rhythms

Nature is full of rhythms. As you accept requests for meetings and appointments, it's a good idea to consider your personal rhythms.

There are two hours each day that I'm able to get a lot done.

The first is the hour before most people arrive in the office. I'm not a morning person, but I find that if I can drag my lazy self into the office an hour early, in that first hour I can get more work done than I can the rest of the day because there's nobody else around. It's important not to waste that hour on things like email. Use it for a project that can't get done without your full attention. (See Chapter 2 for more examples.)

The other hour is your high-energy hour. There is a part of the day that you are able to concentrate better than you can the rest of the day. I call this my "big brain hour." This is a different hour for everyone. For some it is the afternoon, for others it is late at night or early in the morning. This is a real biological phenomenon (Google "circadian rhythms"). NASA uses it to schedule shift work in space missions. Many people take advantage of it to schedule their most difficult tasks during the time of day when they naturally have more energy and ability to concentrate.

Take some time in the next week to find when in the day you are most able to concentrate. You might set your computer to beep once an hour. When you hear it beep, write down on a scale of 0 to 10 your energy level and your ability to concentrate. Find the time that both of them are high.

Once you find a pattern, try to modify your schedule around it.

Schedule your brain work around the time of day when you concentrate the best. Reserve that time for the most important (high-impact) projects. Try to schedule meetings away from that time, unless your meetings require serious brain power. Most don't.

Your high-energy time might change as you grow older. When I was younger, that time for me was right around 2 a.m.; now, it's more like 2 p.m.

Know Your Company's Rhythms

Business is full of rhythms, too. If you identify the rhythms of your company's year, you can make sure your plans are in concert with those rhythms. Anything else is like trying to swim upstream. Your calendar is the long-range planning tool that lets you do this.

Every business has a light time of the year and a heavy time of the year. You can plan your system administration tasks and goals around these patterns.

I used to work at a software company that produced three software releases each year. Every 120 days, a new release would ship. The first month was mostly spent developing marketing requirements and feature lists. There were 60 days of development, two weeks of quality assurance (QA), and two weeks of manufacturing of the software and manuals. Day 120 was shipping day. Then the entire cycle began again. Because it ran like clockwork three times a year, it was a system administrator's dream.

During the first month of the cycle, most of the employees were in meetings and the network was quiet. As long as email was running, nearly any other function could be taken down for maintenance and upgrades. The "tool group" planned which OS/compiler releases would be used for the next version during the last days of the prior release cycle. The first month of the current cycle was when the system administration teams would deploy those tools. During the development stage, outages were tolerated if they were scheduled. Regular system administrator activity could happen. However, toward the end of each 120-day cycle, planned outages were banned. This was a very intense part of the cycle, when new code releases were being shipped to QA almost daily. As a result, this was the best time for system administrators to take time off. A skeleton crew was always around to deal with emergencies, but, otherwise, this is when the system administrators scheduled their vacations. Once the software "went gold" and was in manufacturing, stability was only important in the parts of the system that manufacturing relied on. Everyone else was celebrating. Then the cycle began again.

By planning the system administration work around the company's business cycle, everything went very smoothly.

Another common business cycle is the December holiday rush. For example, it is often true that retailers make half their sales during the holiday shopping season, often losing money the rest of the year. During the holiday rush, the network that supports the business must be completely stable. An hour of downtime can cost millions. Therefore, there is little IT work scheduled for that time. There is plenty of unscheduled work, mostly dealing with emergencies and tuning overloaded servers. Developers are pushed away so that they aren't tempted to make "helpful" changes when the risk would be too big. The busiest time for everyone is often a few months earlier, during the mad rush to get the new systems up and running. The lightest time is the first week of the year, when people most need time to recuperate.

Schools have an obvious cycle. There are projects related to the major milestones of the year: arrival of new students, registration, budget process, finals, graduation, summer.

Hiring has a certain periodic pattern also. For example, if you need to hire entry-level people just out of school, the hiring process often starts by advertising at colleges in February with the hopes of filling jobs with new graduates in May. Similarly, people with more experience might be older and, if they have kids, will want to move between school years, not during. Other factors may affect end-of-the-year hiring. Rarely have I been able to get hiring approval in December, sometimes because the people who approve such things are on vacation, but often because no new hires are permitted so as to keep the end-of-year numbers looking good. Schedule your hiring around these cycles.

I love working in cyclic industries. It makes planning things a lot easier. In fact, when I'm not in a cyclic industry, I try to find the unofficial cycle, or, when possible, move the company into a cycle. One software company I worked at had no consistency in their software releases, and I became the advocate for an *n*-month cycle until one was adopted. The benefits are company-wide: marketing, operations, and budgeting can plan around the cycle, and it nearly eliminates the problem of developers scheduling vacations at inopportune times.

Your company has a similar business cycle. It might be as fast as once a month or as long as a year. If you work at NASA, it might be as long as a multiyear space mission. If you work in politics, it might be as regular as the legislative cycle or the campaign cycle.

Take some time to figure out your company's cycle. You might want to ask your boss what he thinks the business cycle is. Once that is done, consider the following questions:

- What is the business cycle for this company?
- How can I better schedule my projects?
- When is the optimal time to schedule my time off?
- Can the system administration group better schedule its projects?
- Can we turn the system administration processes into cycles that are linked to the light and busy parts of the business cycle?
- If the business pattern is random, can we influence the business to make it more regular? Or can we simply establish a periodic IT schedule and see whether others plan around it?

Summary

- Managing your calendar is important to you and your career. People associate punctuality with responsibility and reliability. People who miss appointments and forget about meetings don't get promotions.
- Without a well-managed calendar, you risk missing important work and nonwork events. It is important to keep balance among work, family life, social life, volunteer work, personal projects, sleep, and so on. Your calendar can help you do that.
- It is important to have a place to write down appointments (or meetings, events, and so on). Write down any appointments that you schedule. Don't agree to an appointment until you've checked your calendar.
- Your calendar fits into The Cycle System by being where you record appointments, dates, milestones, and other information. When you plan your day, you start by using the calendar to plan today's schedule and to add items to today's to do list.

- If you use a PAA, you can organize what you write into each calendar square. I write birthdays and anniversaries at the top, then any vacations and multiday events. I use the middle part of the square to make a mini schedule for the day: morning appointments first, lunch in the middle, and afternoon appointments next. I reserve the very bottom to write my plans for the evening.

- When agreeing to appointments, consider your personal rhythms. If you have the choice, plan brain work during the hours that you are best at focusing.

- When making plans with others, always check your calendar before you agree to the appointment. Don't be embarrassed to make the other person wait for you to find and open your organizer.

- Automate the reminders of appointments. Set alarms on your PDA or use other technology (alarm clocks and so on) if you use a PAA.

- PAA users can record repeating events by making a list of weekly, monthly, and yearly repeating events. On the first day of the week, write the weekly appointments into your calendar. On the first day of the month, write the monthly appointments. On the first day of the year, fill out your yearly repeating events.

- Most companies have a yearly rhythm. For example, retail often has a busy time around December. If you identify the rhythm, you can plan your projects around it. If you don't, you will find yourself swimming upstream. If your company doesn't have a defined rhythm, define one for yourself.

## CHAPTER 7

The Cycle System: Life Goals

At 60, I want to retire and have the financial means to live comfortably.

In the next three years, I want to get promoted to team leader of my group.

In the next month, I want to learn more about Linux kernel internals.

In the next 24 hours, I want to have all my laundry washed and folded.

Someday, I want to date a porn star.

You can achieve anything you want if you set your mind to it. Most people don't follow a logical process of setting goals, figuring out the steps to reach those goals, and then taking those steps. Instead, they expect that things will "just happen."

After becoming extremely efficient in my time management, I realized that I had just spent a year being really good at what I was already doing. However, I was still basically in the same place as I was a year before. I hadn't moved to my dream home, the IT environment I managed hadn't really changed, and I was no closer to dating a porn star. I was spinning my wheels.

The truth is that you will achieve more if you set goals. Studies have found that successful people set goals and work toward them. Recent studies have also found that most unsuccessful people think that if they don't do anything, opportunities will still present themselves. In other words, unsuccessful people hope to be lucky. Hard work beats luck. Friends have told me that chess is a game of luck: the more they practice, the luckier they get. Success is the same way.

However, I'm intrigued by evidence that setting a goal without working toward it is better than not setting goals at all. This makes sense when you think about it. If you haven't determined what your goals are, you can't spot the few opportunities that do cross your path by chance. Suppose your boss asks your team if anyone would like to help planning next year's budget. That sounds like a lot of work with no reward. I'd completely understand if you wanted to avoid it. However, if you had determined that one of your goals was to be promoted to team leader, you would see this as an opportunity to be involved in the long-range planning for the group. If your goal was to move into management, you might see this as an opportunity to see how the budget process works to better prepare you for management. Alternatively, if your goal is to stay technical and prevent any effort by others to promote you into management, this is also an opportunity: it's an opportunity to not accidentally raise your hand! (I've seen too many good technical people accidentally fall into management against their will.)

The techniques covered so far in this book are excellent for getting all those little things done and getting through your day, but what about the big things that take years to achieve?

Begin with the end in mind by asking the big questions:

- What do I want my IT organization to be like two years from now?
- What do I want to have accomplished in my career five years from now?
- Where do I want to be socially and financially 10 years from now?
- What do I want my life to be like when I retire?

The technique here is very simple. You're going to figure out your goals, prioritize them, then work out the steps that will help you reach those goals. Then, you'll turn those steps into to do items and sprinkle them throughout your calendar.

Maybe this is all coming too fast. You're drowning in an endless sea of time management troubles. That's OK. Skim this chapter now, and reread this chapter when you feel you've graduated from the basics.

USER FRIENDLY by Illiad

The Secret Trick

The big secret is to write down your goals. When they are in your head, they aren't as fleshed out as you think they are. They are nebulous. They can't be evaluated, shared with others, or worked on.

The process of writing them down forces you to make them concrete. It's also a lot easier to prioritize a list that is written down.

Written goals can be shared with others. If you have a significant other, you can share your goals with him or her and discuss them. We forget that our loved ones aren't mindreaders. By sharing our goals, we get support and a reality check. We are more likely to achieve a goal if we have told others about it. There's something about telling someone our goals that motivates us to act on them.

It is easy to accidentally write vague goals. You can make a goal significantly more concrete by answering these questions in each goal statement:

- *What* do I want to achieve?
- *When* do I want to have achieved it?

Everyone forgets the when. It's easy to never begin if you don't set a deadline. In the chapter opening, I was careful to include a specific deadline for each goal.

It is also important that goals are measurable. The goals in the chapter opening were mostly measurable. "Living comfortably" could be more specific: a retirement income of 70 percent my current income. Learning "more" about Linux kernel internals isn't measurable. I can fix that by adding a milestone to be achieved, like writing a simple device driver.

 There are other people you might want to consult when setting goals. Your family, religious leaders, boss, neighbors, close friends, and so on. Each person reading this book has a different list of who she thinks is appropriate to consult with. Who is on your list?

In preparation for writing down your goals, take a moment to think about your values. What do you see as your personal mission? Do you believe in helping others or letting others help themselves? Do you want to be rich or happy (or can both be achieved)? Do you value independence or cooperation? Do you value community or self-interest?

Your work-life and home-life values may differ. At home, you may be the nurturing parent, loving all your children equally and helping them to succeed. At work, things may be more competitive or role-oriented.

Setting Goals

How to Get Control of Your Time and Your Life (Signet) is a classic book on time management. The book brings out the necessity of listing your short-, medium-, and long-term goals, and encourages you to categorize them into A, B, and C priorities, with A being the highest priority.

Let's do just that.

Take a big sheet of paper and divide it into six sections, as shown in Figure 7-1 (people with lots of goals or large handwriting might want to use multiple sheets of paper).

	Professional	Personal
1 month		
1 year		
5 years		

Figure 7-1. Goal planning sheet

You're going to fill in each box with a list of life goals in that category. You can add additional timeframes if you feel your goals are grouped differently.

Now spend some time listing your goals. To help you get started, here are some guidelines:

1 month

> Typically these are the smaller projects on your mind. Completing projects that have started, replacing a piece of equipment, and so on.

1 year

> These are the bigger projects. Often they include various reorganizations you'd like to make, both technical ("replace current directory service with a single-sign-on system") or organizational ("reorganize group into customer-focused teams").

5 year

These are the biggest projects, often including life-changing goals such as career moves ("get an MBA and move into management") or life changes ("get married").

Don't worry about their order or whether your goals are good enough for anyone else to see. Just list them. I'll wait.

Really. I'll wait. Don't continue to the next paragraph until you've completed your chart. Not in your head, but on real paper.

You didn't list them did you? You figured you'd come back to this chapter some other time and fill out the table. All the exercises in this book have one thing in common: they don't work unless you do them. So now pull out a sheet of paper and start writing!

I'll wait....

Really....

Are you back? Good.

Now go back and make sure each goal is measurable. Could another person examine the situation and determine that the goal has been met? Can you use numbers or tangible results as evidence of completion? Review your list now and make sure. Again, I'll wait.

Next, for each goal, work out which are As, which are Bs, and which are Cs. As you absolutely must do, Bs are the next most important, and Cs are the good ideas or "would be nice" items that are low priority. This is similar to the priority scheme used in Chapter 4.

Go mark them now. I can't stress enough the importance of doing these exercises as you come across them.

That wasn't as easy as you thought, was it? Did you want to mark everything with an A? I know I did. Prioritization can take as long as, or longer, than writing the initial list.

 You might also want to write "lifetime goals," such as where you want to be when you retire (both geographically and financially). Due to the way compound interest boosts investments, the sooner you start your financial planning, the better.

Planning Your Next Steps

To achieve these goals, you must determine the steps required to get there. You need to break down each goal into the specific tasks that you can write on your to do list. You might want to do this in a word processor so that you can cut and paste into your PDA or print the list and hole-punch it so that it fits in your PAA.

If you aren't sure of the steps, write what you can think of or write down "Research how to do this" and some ideas of where to do the research.

Don't worry about writing the steps in chronological order. Sometimes we have to work backward. You ask yourself, "How would I get there?" and write that step, and then ask yourself, "But how would I have gotten *there*?" and write the step necessary to do that. Eventually, you work backward through the process until you have all the steps you need.

As an example, I'll write my next steps for the goals listed in the beginning of this chapter:

- At 60, I want to retire and have the financial means to live comfortably.
    - Make an appointment with a financial planner.
    - Implement the retirement plan suggested by the planner.
    - Research retirement communities. (How much do they cost? Do they have payment plans? What amenities should I expect?)
    - Research insurance for long-term care facilities or other options in case of Alzheimer's or other situations.
- Within the next three years, I want to get promoted to team leader of my group.
    - Make an appointment with my boss to talk about career goals.
    - Read a book on managing people.
- In the next month, I want to learn more about Linux internals.
    - Ask for recommendations on a sage-members mailing list.
    - Purchase a book.
    - Spend one hour a night reading the book until it's complete.
    - Write a nontrivial program using what I've learned.

- In the next 24 hours, I want to have all my laundry washed and folded.
  - Buy laundry detergent.
  - Wash laundry in washing machine.
  - Move laundry to dryer.
  - Fold and put away laundry.
- I want to date a porn star.
  - Hang out in places where I'm more likely to meet porn stars.
  - Research where such places might be.

(You'll notice some of these steps are in an odd order. As I said, sometimes we work backward.)

These steps aren't written in stone. Often we discover unexpected subgoals along the way. Dorothy wanted to meet the Wizard of Oz so he could help her get home, but as soon as she met him, she learned she had to do a hit job before the return home would be possible. Life is like that.

Schedule the Steps

Now that you know what you want to achieve and the steps that will bring you there, you can sprinkle your next steps throughout your calendar as to do items.

Due to business patterns or family responsibilities, you might have more free time during a certain time of the month or year. Pick the time that you think will most likely assure success. (If you are off by a day, don't worry. The Cycle System will move the steps to the next day.)

Look at the steps you've recorded and consider what the best order should be. Write the first one or two items from each list on the appropriate day's to do list. Let's use "Learn more about Linux internals" as an example. If today is Monday, I write the "Ask for recommendations" step on today's to do list. I should have recommendations by Wednesday, so turn to Wednesday's to do list and write, "Purchase a book based on sage-members recommendations." I'm too cheap to pay for overnight shipping from Amazon, so on the following Monday's to do list, write, "One hour of reading Linux kernel internals book." I write that same item on Tuesday's through Friday's lists, or if I'm using a PDA, I use the "repeating to do item" feature. I don't know how long it will take to read the entire book, but I can set a goal of having done the last item in that list (write a nontrivial program using what I've learned) a week later. If I don't add these items to my to do list, they will never get done.

The 24-hour goal of doing laundry was a joke; it is more of a task than a goal. However, it is a good example of how to link goals to a to do list. I put the first three steps on the place reserved for "after work to do items." I put the last item (fold and put away) on the to do list for the next day.

If you have a lot of goals, this process may seem intimidating. However, this just means that you need to spread your goals out more or downgrade some of the priorities.

It's easy with a PDA to schedule to do items far in advance. However, I find it better to not schedule any single item too far in advance; otherwise, it gets lost. Or I read the item and don't remember what it means. Instead, I schedule the next one, possibly two, steps for each goal. When the step is done, I have a better idea of how much time to allocate for the following steps.

A PAA only has a certain amount of room in it, so you generally only keep the next month of page-per-day sheets in your binder. Therefore, you can't plan your next steps too far in advance. What you can do is mark your next steps in your calendar as you would an appointment. Three months from now, you can "make an appointment" to start a particular step. For example, three months from now you might mark in your calendar, "Research long-term care facilities."

A benefit of this technique is that you don't feel so rushed, but you are still slowly moving toward reaching your various goals.

Take a moment to enter at least one step from each goal into your PDA or organizer.

Revisit Your Goals Regularly

What you have now is a good start. However, you need a way to make sure you keep with the system. On the first day of the month, every month, take a moment to plan your goals. Close your office door (or go to a quiet place) and do the following:

- **Goal review.** Review and update your goal list. Cross out any completed goals. If you've jotted down any new goals since the last goal review, decide if they still sound like good ideas. If they do, prioritize them. Evaluate your prioritization of existing goals vis-à-vis the new goals you've added.

- **Step review.** Review and update your next steps list. As steps are marked "done," schedule later steps into your to do lists, as before.

Over time, you'll get much better at figuring out how to schedule the next steps into your calendar. I try to sprinkle them into Mondays so that when I plan my week, I can make room for them, sliding them to a better day if needed.

How can you remember to do this? Set a repeated event in your PDA called "Goal & Next Step Review." Have it repeat on the first of every month or the first Monday of every month. Now you'll always have a reminder to do this process.

If you use a PAA, set up a sheet of "repeating events" that is reviewed at the start of each month. Every time I load the next month's worth of page-per-day sheets, I go through the "repeating events" sheet and use it to mark the various goal steps in my calendar.

Summary

- To achieve your long-term goals, you need to know what they are and work toward them.
- If you don't write down your goals, you end up spinning your wheels or depending on luck.
- Goals should be measurable: they need a tangible result or numeric measurement that, for example, someone else could check.
- Goals should have deadlines: knowing when a goal should be achieved helps set the pace.
- Begin by listing your one-month, one-year, and five-year goals for work and your life. Prioritize them. List steps required to achieve these goals. Sprinkle the next step of each goal into future to do lists. Once a month, review the goals and steps, reprioritize if needed, and sprinkle more "next steps" into your to do lists.
- Work the next steps as part of your regular to do list management. Gradually, each goal will be achieved or managed.
- Revisit your goals regularly. Add new ones and eliminate old ones. Revise the steps accordingly.

## CHAPTER 8

Prioritization

This is a "bottom up" chapter on setting priorities. First, I'll discuss something I alluded to in Chapter 5: techniques for prioritizing the tasks at hand—today's to do list. Then I'll cover prioritizing bigger things, such as projects. Lastly I'll talk about setting priorities for, or managing, your boss.

USER FRIENDLY by Illiad

Prioritizing Your To Do Lists

There you are at your desk facing today's daily to do list. Dozens of items. How do you decide what to do first?

This section is about prioritizing these items. Different situations call for different schemes. In previous chapters, we used a very simple scheme: if it has to be done today, it's an A priority; if it has to be done soon (but not today), it's a B priority; and everything else is a C priority.

"So what do you do if all your items are A priorities?"

Read this chapter.

Doing Tasks in List Order

System administrators frequently tell me they spend a lot of time each day fretting about what to do next. I know that when I stare at my to do list, I can spend five or more minutes just reading the list, obsessing over which should be the next item to work on. Total up all the time spent wasted that way, and it's a lot of time.

If you are wasting time fretting about what to do next, stop. Make the decision simple and just start at the top of the list and work your way down, doing each item in order. In the time you might spend fretting, you would complete a couple of the smaller items. In addition, because of the way you move items you couldn't complete to the following day, it's common for older items to bubble to the top of the list. Getting these older items done is a great way to start a day.

 One of my chores as a kid was to take out the trash every Monday and Thursday night. I hated it. I would complain and procrastinate and make all sorts of trouble trying to get out of the task. (I think I complained just because that's what kids do when faced with chores.) Though our house was a big, three-story Victorian, it couldn't have taken me more than 10 minutes to empty all the wastebaskets. But what was the fun in that? I had enough delay tactics to waste at least a half-hour before I even got started! There are many situations where just doing the task takes much less time than the efforts we make to avoid the work.

Doing your to do items in the order they appear is a great way to avoid procrastination. To quote the Nike slogan, "Just do it."

If your list is short enough that you can do all the items in one day, then this scheme makes even more sense. If it doesn't matter if a task gets done early in the day or late in the day, who cares in what order it's completed?

This is very much like network congestion. If a network is lightly loaded it's easy to do audio, video, telephony, or other time-critical services. However, with a congested network, these services work a lot better with some kind of sophisticated prioritization scheme, or quality of service (QoS) system. When the network load is light, any scheme will work. When the network load is heavy, we need something more structured. When our task list is simple, any prioritization scheme will work. When we are flooded with requests, we need something more sophisticated.

To extend my analogy a little further, did you know that QoS often isn't about treating some packets better? It's really about treating some packets worse! Technically, what's going on inside a QoS switch is very interesting. When there is no congestion, it operates the same as a non-QoS switch. Packets come in, packets go out. However, when congestion happens, a non-QoS switch simply drops the most recently arrived packet. In other words, there's no buffer space left for a new packet, so it ignores that packet. A QoS-enabled switch handles congestion differently. When the buffer is full, it doesn't drop the newly arrived packet; instead, it picks a lower-priority packet in the "middle" of the buffer to drop. In other words, when you pay an ISP for better QoS on certain traffic, you are really paying to not be dropped during congestion. You are literally bribing the ISP to drop someone else's packet when the network is congested!

Task prioritization is similar. We have a finite amount of time and resources. When we are overloaded, we have a tendency to growl at the next new request we get. In reality, we need a way to look at our current task list and decide if there are lower-priority items to delay or possibly drop. (Sadly, we can't take bribes!)

Prioritizing Based on Customer Expectations

Here's a little secret I picked up from Ralph Loura when he was my boss at Bell Labs. If you have a list of tasks, doing them in any order takes (approximately) the same amount of time. However, if you do them in an order that is based on customers' expectations, your customers will perceive you as working faster. Same amount of work for you, better perception from your customers. Pretty cool, huh?

What are your customer expectations? Sure, all customers would love all requests to be completed immediately, but, in reality, they do have some concept that things take time. It may be an unrealistic expectation, and certainly it is often based on a misunderstanding of technology, but we can place user expectations in a few broad categories:

- **Some requests should be quick.** Examples include resetting a password, requests to allocate an IP address, and deleting a protected file. One thing these requests have in common is that they are often minor tasks that hold up a larger task. Imagine the frustration a user experiences when she can't do anything until a password is reset, but you take hours before doing it.

- **"Hurry up and wait" tasks will start soon.** Tasks that are precursors to other tasks are expected to happen early on. For example, ordering a small hardware item usually involves a lot of work to push the order through purchasing, then a long wait for it to arrive. After that, the item can be installed. If the wait is going to be two weeks, there is an expectation that the ordering will happen quickly so that the two-week wait won't stretch into three weeks.

- **Some requests take a long time.** Examples include installing a new PC, creating a service from scratch, or anything that requires a purchasing process. Even if the vendor offers overnight shipping, people accept that overnight is not right now.

- **All other work stops to fix an outage.** The final category is outages. Not only is there an expectation that during an outage all other work will stop so the issue can be resolved, there is also an expectation that the entire team will work on the project. Customers generally do not know that there is a division of labor within an SA team.

Now that you understand your customers' expectations better, how can you put this to good use? Let's suppose you had the tasks in Figure 8-1 on your to do list.

Task	Description	Expectation	Actual work	Time completed
T1	Reset password	1 minute	10 minutes	9:10 a.m.
T2	Create new user account	Next day	20 minutes	9:30 a.m.
T3	Install new server	Next day	4 hours (+1 for lunch)	2:30 p.m.
T4	Add new CGI area to web server	1 hour	30 minutes	3:00 p.m.
T5	Order a software package	1 hour	1 hour	4:00 p.m.
T6	Debug minor NetNews error	10 minutes	25 minutes	4:25 p.m.
T7	Allocate IP address	2 minutes	5 minutes	4:30 p.m.

Figure 8-1. Tasks that aren't prioritized by customer expectations

If you did the tasks in the order listed, you could be pretty satisfied with your performance. You did everything on the day it was requested—6.5 hours of solid work (plus one hour for lunch). Good for you.

However, you have not done a good job of meeting your customer's perception of how long things should have taken. The person who made request T7 had to wait all day for something he perceived should take two minutes. If I were that customer, I would be pretty upset. For the lack of an IP address, the installation of a new piece of lab equipment was delayed all day.

(Actually, what's more likely to happen is that the frustrated, impatient customer wouldn't wait all day. He'll ping IP addresses until he finds one that isn't in use—at that moment—and temporarily borrow that address. If this is your unlucky day, the address selected will conflict with something and cause an outage, which could ruin your entire day. But I digress....)

Let's reorder the tasks based on customer perception of how long things should take. Tasks that are perceived to take little time will be batched up and done early in the day. Other tasks will happen later. However, you will make one exception to the rule, as you'll soon see. Figure 8-2 shows the reordered tasks.

Task	Description	Expectation	Actual work	Time completed
T1	Reset password	1 minute	10 minutes	9:10 a.m.
T7	Allocate IP address	2 minutes	5 minutes	9:15 a.m.
T5	Order a software package	1 hour	1 hour	10:15 a.m.
T4	Add new CGI area to web server	1 hour	30 minutes	10:45 a.m.
T2	Create new user account	Next day	20 minutes	11:05 a.m.
T3	Install new server	Next day	4 hours (+1 for lunch	4:05 p.m.
T6	Debug minor NetNews error	10 minutes	25 minutes	4:30 p.m.

Figure 8-2. Tasks ordered based on customer expectations

You begin the day by doing the two tasks (T1 and T7) that customers expect to happen quickly and that most certainly will hold up other, larger projects. You succeed in meeting the perceived amount of time these tasks take.

The next task (T5) involves a "hurry up and wait" situation. No matter how quickly you order the item, it is going to take a day or two to arrive. Putting the order through sooner rather than later can prevent a lot of dissatisfaction on the other end.

Your next task (T4) is done in 30 minutes. Check.

Task T2 doesn't take very long, but the expectation for a new user account to be created is usually not measured in minutes and hours, but in deadlines. If the person's first day on the job is tomorrow, it is expected that her accounts will be created before she arrives, whether it takes one minute or one day, whether you do it early or late in the day. However, since the task is deadline driven, it is important that it gets done.

If there were an outage (caused, possibly, by two hosts being configured for the same IP address), and all work stops to fix an outage, the previously outlined schedule would be disrupted. However, I would still work to meet the expectation that the new account be created before the person arrived. Other tasks might be delayed for a day, which is understandable given the major outage. But for a task like creating an account, I would stay late rather than miss the deadline.

Installing a new server (T3) is one of those "black hole tasks." It should take a few minutes to mount the server in the rack, maybe an hour to load the operating system, a little longer to configure the system. At least vendors seem to think that's true. We system administrators know that it's never that easy. The first time you rack mount that particular product, it always takes hours to figure out the oddball mounting system the vendor has created. Server operating systems are often loaded, erased, loaded, erased, as you carefully adjust settings each time to get things just right. (This box is going to be around for years, so we might as well invest some time in getting things right.) Finally, configuration never goes as quickly as we hope it will. Therefore, we leave these black hole tasks until after we've completed the tasks that are expected to happen quickly.

We bent the prioritization rules for the last task (T6). Based on the expected time for completion, one would think I'd have done it earlier in the day, perhaps before or after T3. However, at every site I've worked at, Usenet NetNews is considered a low priority, recreational activity provided as a bonus to employees. (I've never worked at an ISP, where the situation may be different.) Thus, fixing a minor issue with it is a low priority and goes to the end of the list. The general rule is: when all parties agree that a task is low priority (or there is a management edict), move the task to the end of the list. Think of it this way: if someone complained that one of the other tasks wasn't completed, would you want to stand in front of your boss and explain that the customer's request was delayed because you were fixing a minor issue with Usenet? No, not at all.

Simple? Sure. It can take a little practice, but your customers will notice the difference.

Delegate, record, do revisited

When I explain this system to people, the main objection I hear from them is that their to do list is not static. They do not begin their day with a fixed list of things that need to be done. New items are added to their list all day.

That's why we use the delegate, record, do technique from Chapter 2 for dealing with interruptions. We can use our customers' expectations to influence which of these three actions we take.

A request for resetting a password should happen quickly because it's holding up other work. Therefore, it might be faster to do it than to delegate it to someone else. And you certainly don't want to record the task for later when it means delaying a person's entire schedule.

Mutual interruption shield revisited

Not only does this technique work for prioritizing your personal to do list, but you can use it to plan on a larger scale. Use it to organize your entire computer support department!

Remember the mutual interruption shield technique from Chapter 1? Essentially, you implement this system to make sure that people's expectations are matched. Your coworker catches all interrupts for half of the day so that you can get projects done, and you reverse roles for the other half of the day. What you're really doing is making sure that there is someone to do the tasks that customers expect will happen quickly.

Most helpdesks have Tier 1 members who answer the phone and only push an issue to the Tier 2 staff when they are stumped. This is, essentially, creating a mutual interruption shield for the entire team while providing response times that match customer expectations!

Prioritizing based on customer expectations and using the mutual interruption shield replicates the helpdesk tier system, which validates the combination. Or, one might say that the tier structure is validated by the fact that it aims to reach the goal of meeting customer expectations. Either way, it's pretty cool, huh?

Project Priorities

The previous sections described ways to prioritize individual tasks. Now I'll present some useful techniques for prioritizing projects.

Prioritization for Impact

Let's say that you and your fellow SAs brainstormed 20 great projects to do next year. However, you only have the budget and people to accomplish a few of them. Which projects should you pick?

In general, I find I get better results when I choose projects on a "biggest impact first" basis.

It's tempting to pick the easy projects and do them first. You know how to do them, and there isn't much controversy around them, so at least you'll know that they'll be completed.

It's very tempting to pick out the fun projects, or the politically safe projects, or the projects that are the obvious next steps based on past projects.

Ignore those temptations and find the projects that will have the biggest positive impact on your organization's goals. In fact, I assert that it is better to do one big project that will have a large, positive impact than many easy projects that are superficial. I've seen it many times. An entire team working on one goal works better than everyone having a different project. This is because we work better when we work together.

Here's another way to look at it. All projects can fit into one of the four categories listed in Figure 8-3.

	Easy (small effort)	Difficult (big effort)
Big positive impact	A	B
Superficial impact	C	D

Figure 8-3. Project impact versus effort

It's obvious to do category A first. An easy project that will have a big impact is rare, and when such a project magically appears in front of us, it's obvious to do it. (Warning: be careful, a project's A status may be a mirage.)

It's also obvious to avoid category D projects. A project that is difficult and won't change much shouldn't be attempted.

However, most projects are either in category B or C and it is human nature to be drawn to the easy C projects. You can fill your year with easy projects, list many accomplishments, and come away looking very good. However, highly successful companies train their management to reward workers who take on category B projects—the difficult but necessary ones.

Once you think about it in terms of return on investment (ROI), it makes sense. You are going to spend a certain amount of money this year. Do you spend it on many small projects, each of which will not have a big impact? No, you look at the biggest positive impact and put all your investment into that effort.

It is important to make sure these big impact projects are aligned with your company's goals. It is important for the company and important for you, too. You will be more valued that way.

Requests from Your Boss

If your boss asks you to do something, and it's a quick task (not a major project), do it right away. For example, if your boss asks you to find out approximately how many PCs use the old version of Windows, get back to him with a decent estimate in a few minutes.

It helps to understand the big picture. Usually such requests are made because your boss is putting together a much larger plan or budget and you can hold up your boss's entire day by not getting back to him with an answer quickly. Perhaps he is working out the staffing and cost estimates to bring all PCs up to the latest release of Windows. The entire project would be held up while waiting for your answer.

Why does this matter? Well, your boss decides your next salary review. Do I need to say more?

Maybe I do. Your boss will have a fixed amount of money he can dole out for all raises. If he gives more to Moe, then Larry is going to get less. When your boss is looking at the list of people in the team, do you want him to look at your name and think, "He sure did get me an estimate of the number of out-of-date Windows quickly. Gosh, he always gets me the things I need quickly." Or, do you want your boss to be thinking, "You know, the entire budget was held up for a day because I was waiting for that statistic." Or worse yet, "All the times I looked foolish in front of my boss because of a missed deadline, it was because I was waiting for so-and-so to get me a piece of information. So-and-so isn't getting a good raise this year."

Managing Your Boss

Many people think that management is a one-way street. I disagree. Management is a relationship, and you share influence in how the relationship evolves. It is difficult to get anything done, or to have a satisfying career, if you do not have a good relationship with your manager. Alternatively, with a good relationship you can get more done, have increased job satisfaction, and accelerate your career.

If you do a web search for "manage your boss," you will find many excellent articles. This is a sign that many people feel the need to have a better relationship with their boss. Schedule some time to read a few of them.

I think the three most important keys to managing your boss are to use him to help advance your career, to know when to use upward delegation, and to understand and contribute to his goals.

Make sure your boss knows your career goals

Make sure your boss knows where you want to be two, five, or ten years from now. Your boss doesn't have ESP. In fact, if you are doing your job well, he may be hoping that you want to stay right where you are. It's less chaotic for him if everyone just wants to stay put. But that's not your career goal, right? You want to move into a more senior role, or move into management, or possibly you are just doing this job until you've saved enough money to pay your bills while you struggle to become a full-time artist, actor, or author.

The key is to make sure that your boss knows your goals. So, tell him your goals and dreams. Don't be shy, but don't sound like a broken record. Once a year you should discuss, in a private one-on-one meeting, where you want your career to go. I remember the day I walked into Les Lloyd's office and said, "Les, I may be a freshman now, but someday I want to be one of the student managers here at the computer center." He thought for a moment and told me what accomplishments I needed to have under my belt before he would consider me for the position. I worked my ass off that summer and soon he announced my promotion. I have had similar experiences at jobs after graduation.

Upward delegate only when it leverages your boss's authority

Upward delegation means giving an action item to your boss. The key is to know when to do it and when not to. If you try to give your boss an action item when it isn't appropriate, it looks like you are avoiding doing your work.

Here's an appropriate case: you are having trouble convincing a customer that her department has to pay for a server. Either she wants your IT team to pay for it, or she doesn't feel that the server is needed. Asking your boss to help explain the situation to her is appropriate because it leverages his authority. He has the authority to speak to the business issues involved, while your credentials are relevant to technical aspects. Your boss's authority also leverages his knowledge of the political power structure of your organization. He may know that it is a lost cause, or whether it would be appropriate to go over the customer's head.

Solve Problems at the Right Level

Don't debate technical issues with vice presidents, and don't solve a political issue with technology.

Managers usually want to speak to people at their level. Vice presidents generally communicate with other vice presidents. Directors generally communicate best with other directors. If you need to cross this line, communicate to the peer who reports to the person you want to speak with, or go through your boss, who is much more able to navigate the organizational structure.

To clarify this point, let's look at a situation where it would not be appropriate to upward delegate. The server has been purchased and is waiting to be installed. Would it be appropriate to ask your boss to install it? Generally, the answer is no. Such a task does not leverage his authority. If he is technical, he may have more experience and be able to install the server faster than you, but if he has delegated it to you, trying to push it back up to him simply looks like you are shirking your responsibility.

On the other hand, if you do not know how to install such a server, asking for help is appropriate. In that case, you are not asking for your boss to do the task, you are asking for training. It *is* leveraging his authority to ask for training. A manager's primary responsibility is to allocate resources. He can decide whether it is appropriate to train you personally or delegate the task to a coworker. By asking him for training, you are making a request that is appropriate because you are asking for the allocation of training resources.

Understand and help accomplish your boss's goals

If you want your manager to help you, you have to help him. "But why? It's his job to do things like career management, right?" Well, technically yes, but you get more flies with honey than vinegar. Your manager will spend more energy making you a success if it's obvious that you spend time making him a success.

More specifically, success in this case means meeting your boss's goals. Earlier I wrote that you shouldn't expect your boss to have ESP and be able to guess your career goals. Likewise, don't try to use your ESP to guess your boss's goals. More experienced coworkers might have a good understanding of what motivates your boss, and you should listen to them for guidelines. However, nothing beats talking directly to your boss.

I've had a number of bosses who surprised me when, privately, I asked them what their goals were and how I could help them meet those goals. The way I phrased my query was something like: "What metrics does your boss use to evaluate your performance? If I know how you are measured, I can contribute to the team more effectively by keeping those goals in mind."

In one case, my boss explained to me the specific technical projects he wanted to see completed that year. He had "sold" these projects to management, and they were expecting them to be completed. I soon realized that much of the work I did had little to do with those projects, and I redirected my priorities to make my boss a success. He noticed, and I benefited.

Another time, I was told the criteria that determined whether my boss got a bonus at the end of the year. It sounded greedy at first, but then I realized, who am I to judge? So I redirected my priorities to make sure that those criteria were met. My goal was, essentially, to make sure my boss's bonus was maximized. That would put me in the best position to get what I wanted, whether it was a raise, a promotion, or just a super-duper cool new computer on my desk. Is this unethical? Certainly not (as long as I didn't do anything unethical to meet those goals, of course).

This brings up an interesting conundrum. What if my boss had said the criteria he was measured by was something that I felt wasn't good for the company? For example, if I felt that what the company needed most was to strive for technical excellence, but he was being measured by growth metrics? You have to trust the judgment of the superiors who set up your boss's criteria. Or, strive for both goals. Sound difficult? Well, if you're smart enough to know more about what's right for your company than your boss's boss, it shouldn't be very difficult to find a way to meet both goals at the same time.

I don't think it's cynical to give higher management exactly what they ask for. However, sometimes your boss is measured in a way that unintentionally promotes bad behavior. For example, I once visited an IT helpdesk whose manager was rewarded based on whether he was able to decrease the average initial response time to customer requests. (You can see where this is going, right?) Soon, everyone he managed was answering calls on the first ring (or very soon after receiving an electronic trouble ticket) and putting the caller on hold. Service wasn't getting any better, but they were meeting their metrics. The following year, management started measuring performance based on average time to resolution. As you can guess, tickets were closed very quickly whether or not the issue was really resolved. The statement, "I'll close this ticket; you reopen it if my suggestion didn't fix your problem" became commonplace. Again, customer satisfaction didn't improve.

If management thinks the only way to drive a business is on metrics, but is incompetent at creating metrics that successfully encourage the desired behavior, then they should either learn how to make better metrics or not manage using metrics.

 A friend once worked at an ISP that measured the sales team based on T1's booked, with no penalty if the order was cancelled later. The boss encouraged everyone to get customers to sign contracts and cancel when the technician came to perform the installation. Unethical? Maybe at first, but after more than a year of this, the management that set up the criteria didn't change the criteria. Therefore, they must not have seen this as a problem, right? The boss, and his staff, enjoyed a long string of bonuses for meeting their superiors' goals. Did the ISP eventually go out of business? Absolutely. The Internet is a better place for having one fewer ISP with incompetent management.

A friend asked his boss what his boss's goals were and was completely surprised by what his boss revealed. His boss was getting near retirement and really just wanted a quiet last year with no surprises. He was, essentially, told not to work very hard for the next year because work meant new projects, and new projects meant new risks. The boss really just wanted to sail through to his last day. My friend realized he had three choices: (1) have a relaxing year, (2) work hard to position himself for a promotion to succeed his boss, or (3) update his resume and start job hunting. He chose the first option. It was his most enjoyable year at the company. He spent the time sending himself to various kinds of training conferences and workshops. Coincidentally, the training positioned him for a promotion. After his boss retired, he was promoted to replace his boss. I guess it all worked out in the end.

When you visibly contribute to making your boss a success, it opens many doors. He will spend extra effort helping you with your career path, you will increasingly receive first pick at the "fun" projects, and it opens the possibilities to small but important rewards such as cool equipment. Of course, it can't hurt your potential to receive better raises and bonuses. Best of all, if your boss is successful enough to receive a promotion, an ethical boss will take you with him.

From that perspective, the ultimate criterion for how to prioritize your work is to center it around what will make your boss a success.

Action expresses priorities.

—Mahatma Gandhi

Summary

- When you have a lot to do, prioritization becomes more important. When you have more to do than you have time for, prioritization is extremely important. When you have very little to do, any prioritization scheme works pretty well.

- Doing tasks in order works fine when you have a small number of tasks. Since older items bubble up to the top of the list, they will tend to get done. This is a good scheme to use when you are otherwise at a loss for what to do. Doing the first task on your list is better than spending time fretting about which task to do first.

- Prioritizing based on customer expectation means first doing the tasks that customers expect will be done quickly. Customers expect small requests to be done quickly if the problem will delay their larger projects. You spend the same amount of time working and have more satisfied customers when you prioritize this way.

- When deciding which projects should have higher priority, base the decision on impact. A high-impact project that requires a large effort to complete will benefit you more than a low-impact project that is easy to achieve.

- Requests from your boss should have special priority. Your boss's requests often have dependencies that you are unaware of. Don't be the reason his larger project is delayed!

- To manage your boss, you must do three things: make sure your boss knows your career goals, use upward delegation only when it leverages his authority, and understand his goals and be part of accomplishing them. When you do these three things, you are in better sync with your boss, and he becomes more flexible with your requests because he knows that you have his best interest in mind.

## CHAPTER 9

Stress Management

Stressed? Of course you are! You're a system administrator!

I'm not a doctor, and I'm not an expert on stress, but I will share with you what little I've learned over the years. I'm quite a stress puppy—ask anyone I've worked with. However, I think I manage it better than I used to.

This chapter is about some common sources of stress and what to do about them, some advice about vacation time, and a little story about how I learned to relax. It is advice that I've found myself giving time and time again, sometimes when lecturing on the road or when socializing with fellow system administrators or coworkers. A lot of this is more philosophy than science. It is not a complete or scholarly discourse on the subject, but it should give you some useful advice and point you in the right direction to find more information.

Stress is the wear and tear that our bodies and minds feel when things change. There is positive stress and negative stress. Positive stress adds anticipation and excitement to our lives, helps us be creative, helps us win a race or an election, or pushes us beyond what we previously thought were our limits. Negative stress is destructive. It causes heart disease, depression, and gray hairs. Managing stress is a big part of maintaining good mental health.

Oddly enough, the same situation can be positive stress for one person and negative stress for another. It's all about how we deal with it. For example, people have different reactions to compliments from a manager. For some, such a thing would be good. Others might have the opposite reaction. They might think, "Oh, now I'll always be expected to be so successful! I can't handle the pressure!" They might think, "He said that in front of everyone. Now they all hate me!" and worry that the rest of the group might be jealous and vengeful.

It is not what happens to us that causes stress, it is how we react to what happens to us. I've found *Feeling Good: The New Mood Therapy* (Collins) and *The Feeling Good Handbook* (Plume) to be extremely helpful and highly regarded books in the area of managing stress in productive ways. Many people have turned their lives around with the help of these books.

We must work hard at relaxing so that we get good at it. We have to intentionally set aside time to relax and develop the discipline to not postpone it. It's mental hygiene. You can skip brushing your teeth now and then, but in the long run you will suffer. Similarly, you can skip the things you do for mental hygiene now and then, but in the long run you will suffer. The more you practice relaxation, the better you get at it.

The smokers I know all seem to be so relaxed at work. I don't think it's all about the nicotine. I think it's the fact that they take themselves out of the office every couple hours (we don't permit smoking inside the building). That breaks up the day. Stress builds a little, then is reduced by going outside. Their stress builds, then they go outside. I'm not recommending smoking, but I do encourage you to go outside every couple of hours, stretch your legs, and get some perspective.

USER FRIENDLY by Illiad

Overload and Conflicting Directions

As a system administrator, I find my two biggest sources of stress are feeling overloaded and being given conflicting directions from management.

When I feel overloaded, I remind myself about the techniques for to do list management in Chapter 5. I close my office door (or steal a conference room), get some peace, and focus on The Cycle techniques. Soon, I realize that what got me feeling overloaded was that I was skipping steps. I go through the steps and plan the remainder of my day, moving to do items to the next day, and so on. It feels good to manage all of my tasks.

When I'm *really* overloaded, that doesn't work, and I have to seek a higher power, most particularly my boss. A good boss can help prioritize your workload when you are overloaded. It is not a weakness to confess that you are overloaded. Asking for help is a sign of strength. It takes a lot of courage to ask for help, and even more to accept the advice offered.

If your boss isn't around, anyone can help. Explaining the situation to someone can really help with the stress. Even if they don't have any advice, at least you feel like you've been heard. Often that's half the battle. Being heard by others feels good. However, they usually do have advice or can give you reassurance about the things that are unsettling. That always makes me feel better.

The act of explaining something out loud to someone helps us solve our own problems. How many times have you realized the solution to a problem while explaining it to someone else? Life is full of those moments when you tell someone, "So there's this problem, see? If I...." Suddenly you realize the answer, and there is no need to continue talking. It happens all the time.

The Practice of Programming (Addison Wesley) tells the story of one person at Bell Labs who was known for helping many people solve their highly technical problems. Sadly, he couldn't always stop what he was doing to listen to someone, so he had a teddy bear in his office. When he was busy, he would tell people to "talk to the bear." It worked very well. Soon he found people stopping by his office and going straight to the bear.

Detecting when you are so stressed that you need to pause and use these techniques can be a problem. When I'm super-stressed, I'm not able to recognize that this is the exact time to stop what I'm doing and destress. I once had an arrangement with a coworker where we had a code word we would use that would mean, "You're too stressed to see how stressed you are." It was a code word so that it could be said in front of others without embarrassment. He did it for me and I did it for him. It was very helpful.

Receiving conflicting directions is another common stressor for system administrators. Often, system administrators have more than one boss. Each boss gives you conflicting priorities. You try your best to please both, which is fine until you get overloaded.

In a perfect world, you can get both bosses into a room and let them duke it out. Sadly, that isn't always possible. If you are able to make that happen, it is a good idea to have your bosses write out your priorities so that you can refer to it the next time there is a conflict. Of course, if you have to refer to this memorandum of understanding too much, it may be better to seek out an organizational change that fixes the root cause of the problem. You might also consider talking to your favorite of the two bosses about working exclusively for him or her.

The inability to resolve such an issue is one of the leading causes of system administrators seeking employment elsewhere. And for good reason. Maybe a good stress reliever is to update your resume and read the employment section of a newspaper.

Sleep Mitigates Stress

Adequate sleep fixes a slew of problems. Everyone is different and needs a different amount of sleep. Getting the right amount helps you deal with stress better.

During a particularly stressful week, I find that if I get an extra hour of sleep I'm able to manage stress better. I feel better, I'm more relaxed, and I get along with people easier.

The problem is that getting an extra hour of sleep is difficult. We usually can't sleep an hour late, so our only choice is to go to sleep an hour earlier. That's hard! There's so much good TV to watch, books to read, chatrooms to play in, web sites to visit, games to play, and so on.

The only way I'm able to get myself into bed earlier is with a little help. I ask my significant other to be involved (in other words, force me to do it). If you don't have a significant other, have a friend call and nag you. Or, set an alarm that can ring to remind you to go to sleep.

I can't just go to sleep earlier. It's a process. I have to do nothing for a half-hour to wind down enough to be ready to sleep. It's pretty difficult for me to do nothing, but I usually get there in about 15 minutes. I think of it as a countdown. At T-120, I stop eating or drinking. At T-30, I wash up. At T-15, I start doing nothing. At T-0, I turn off the lights and crawl into bed. At T+5 I'm...zzzzzzz.

Vacation Time

Let me tell you a little secret about vacation time.

Companies don't give you time off because they want to be nice to you. They aren't doing it to be charitable.

They're doing it because you're difficult to work with when you are stressed. Let me say that a little more forcefully: when you postpone taking time off, you become a pain in the ass to everyone in the office, and we don't like working with you. You're irritable, difficult, and disagreeable. SO TAKE TIME OFF, DAMN IT!

Sorry for yelling, but it's for your own good.

A successful vacation takes your mind off work enough so that it can relax. It may take several days to forget about work enough so that you are in full relaxation mode. Only then can your body repair itself. I need at least three days to get to relaxation mode, and then six or more days of relaxation to really feel refreshed. Add a couple travel days and a day to get back into the swing of things, and we're talking 12 to 14 days for a really successful vacation. You deserve at least as much.

Let's look at some common vacation mistakes that system administrators make:

- **Using an occasional vacation day to run errands, do laundry, etc.** That's not a vacation. That's using vacation time, but it doesn't meet the goal of relaxing. Maybe you can use comp time for errands or come into work early and take an hour or two off during the day to run errands.

- **Taking a long weekend.** That's sort of like a vacation, but it skips the multiday process of getting to relaxation mode. Plus, when I try this, I end up with a backlog of weekend chores. That creates even more stress. A series of long weekends doesn't count either.

- **Bringing your laptop and checking email every few hours while on vacation.** If you check email during your vacation, you never really relax. Every time you check your email you put your brain back in work mode and you need another three days to return to relax mode. Most hotels provide Internet access for a small charge. I want a hotel that, for a small charge, promises that I will be completely prevented from getting anywhere near any kind of Internet access.

Not checking email is difficult. Very difficult. When I take a real vacation I have to coordinate to have my VPN access shut off, or I will not be able to prevent myself from reading email. It's a sickness.

The first few days of a vacation I tend to have work on my mind. I find that if I'm having trouble letting go, it can be useful to write down what's on my mind so that it will be there when I return to work. Otherwise, I'll try to keep the idea in my brain, and that just prevents me from letting go.

I've heard system administrators brag about not taking vacation. "This company can't survive without me! I'm proud that I haven't had a vacation in years." I cringe when I hear this. As a manager, I fear an SA may develop a martyr complex. A person with a *martyr complex* assumes that because she is paying such a great price to keep the company running, everyone owes her something. She becomes impossible to work with. I find that a person in this situation eventually feels overwhelmed, cornered, and unable to escape. The person who feels this way typically leaves the company soon, often unexpectedly, and I lose a technically talented person who is difficult to replace.

 I feel less cornered when I can leave a job easily and without guilt. Keeping good documentation helps that. Chapter 12 explains how to make it easier to document processes.

A long vacation has another business benefit—it helps determine where your coverage and/or documentation is lacking. Good system administrators assume that they may be hit by a truck tomorrow and the company should be able to continue without them. Taking a long vacation is one way to test that theory without suffering bodily harm.

Here's my advice about taking a vacation:

- Two weeks before you leave, figure out what coverage is needed and spend time training the person who is covering for you.
- The week before you leave, make sure that the person can do those tasks without asking questions.
- The day before you leave, do not do anything as root or Administrator. You don't want to make any changes that can't be fixed. If the temptation is great, distract yourself: spend the day writing documentation.
- When you return, take time to see where the coverage gaps occurred. It is common to find that something stopped working and that your company lived without it until you returned. What was it that broke? What could have been documented?

"But how could I ever train someone to know *everything* that I know?" You don't have to. He only has to know enough so that your company can survive a week or two. For example, maybe one of your jobs is to generate a certain set of reports each week. The person who covers for you doesn't have to know how to create new report templates, just how to run the ones that exist. If a new report template is needed, it can wait until you get back. If it is a real emergency, people can print out a few reports and cut and paste the bits of paper into the format they need. (In reality, the person who needs the report will understand because she takes vacations, too.)

Here's another example: maybe you are in charge of backups. The person covering for you needs to know how to do any daily tape changes and how to restore a deleted file or directory. He doesn't need to know how to add a new disk volume to the schedule or how to readjust the schedule. It is unlikely that a new disk will be added to the system while you are away, and if some manager has a brilliant new backup schedule she'd like to see implemented, waiting another week should be fine. Of course, if a catastrophic failure happened and RAID or other failover systems weren't able to save the data, you might have to come back from vacation early, but how often does that happen? (And if it would result in losing millions of dollars per day, why is only one person trained in your disaster-recovery process? But I digress....)

When you have someone trained to cover for you, it's important to make sure that you coordinate vacations so that you both aren't out at the same time. This is a normal business practice. In fact, at most companies I know, the CEO coordinates time off with the CFO, and the VP of engineering coordinates with a direct report. We are at least as important and should do the same.

Yoga, Meditation, and Massage

From an early age I had bizarre misconceptions about yoga, meditation, and massage. I thought they were strange things that should be ignored. How wrong I was! They are all excellent techniques for relaxing the body and mind. They are important parts of a good relaxation and stress management program to maintain top mental health.

But before I go on, let me embarrass myself by telling you what I thought they were:

- **Yoga.** I thought yoga was some kind of weird exercise that people did to become more flexible. Bad experiences with gymnastics at an early age convinced me that I could never be flexible, so I ignored yoga. Why would I need to be physically flexible?

- **Meditation.** I thought meditation was some kind of religious thing. In particular, something that wasn't part of my religion, so I turned a blind eye to the topic (or should I say a blind third eye?).

- **Massage.** I had two conflicting misconceptions about massage. The first was that I thought it was some kind of self-indulgent pampering that rich people did. I ain't rich, so I ignored it out of hand. Second, as a young child, I saw Peter Sellers play the role of a masseur on *The Muppet Show*. He twisted Kermit's body in all sorts of crazy ways. I couldn't understand why anyone would subject himself to that.

It's funny how early impressions stay with us for so long.

When I was in my mid-20s, I signed up for a class on relaxation that met one night a week for eight weeks. I wouldn't have taken it if I knew it was going to teach things like yoga, meditation, and massage. As I said, those were "weird" things that I ignored. They tricked me!

The idea of the class was to give people a taste of various techniques. It wasn't expected that everyone would enjoy all of them. However, if there was a single one that worked well for you, you could explore that further. Sort of like the fried appetizer special at Denny's.

Here's what I learned:

- **Yoga.** Yoga is the practice of an ancient discovery concerning relaxation. By putting your body in certain positions and holding those positions, the body relaxes. The muscles relax. When that happens—the mind relaxes. Who knew?

- **Meditation.** Meditation is an intentional quieting of the mind. If you can shut out all other noise and thoughts, your mind can relax and your body will follow. The better you get at it, the more amazing it gets. Oh, how wrong I had been.

- **Massage.** Massage is the physical manipulation of the muscles to relax them. I have back pains, and it was quite amazing to learn that it's not my back that hurts, it's the muscles in my back getting so tight that they hurt. They don't relax (loosen) all the way because of the pain, which means they stay tight, which hurts. That pain makes them tighten more, and the cycle builds on itself. Massage relaxes the muscles and brings them to a calm, relaxed state. I find that a monthly massage keeps my muscles from ever getting too tight (sort of similar to how rebooting Windows servers once a month helps them stay fresh).

I bring all this up because maybe you have been avoiding these things because of misconceptions. I encourage you to explore these techniques. Trying them for yourself is the only way to find out if you like them. You probably won't find all of them appealing. However, only one needs to work for you.

There are centers all over the country that offer such training. They usually advertise in holistic healing or naturally living catalogs that you might find in your local health food store. Places such as Omega Institute in Rhinebeck, New York (near Woodstock; *http://www.eomega.com*) have introductory weekends that are an excellent starting point. Your local YMCA, community college, or high school adult program may also have resources. Ask around.

Summary

- System administration is a stressful job. Therefore, managing stress well is part of doing your job well.

- Often, the causes of stress that are most pressing are the feeling of being overloaded and of being pulled in multiple directions by multiple bosses with different priorities.

- Feeling overloaded can be greatly helped by time management techniques, especially The Cycle System.

- Stress caused by conflicting priorities needs to be fixed at the root of the problem by maintaining communication with the sources of the conflict or by bringing the involved parties into the same room at the same time for dialog.

- Relaxation is something that can be managed and practiced. You can manage it by setting aside time to purposefully relax with techniques like yoga, meditation, and massage.

- You need to work hard at relaxing so that you get good at it. Just as it takes time to change the oil in your car, you must set aside time to intentionally relax.

- Vacation time is not a gift from your employer. It is part of your relaxation regiment and stress-reduction program. It is what you do to maintain your mental health. Postponing vacation time is like postponing brushing your teeth. It may seem convenient to skip it now, but in the long term it is not healthy. If you squander your vacation time by using it for a day off to run errands, it does not serve its stress-reduction purpose.

- I hate to be gruesome, but good SAs assume that a truck may hit them tomorrow and the company should be able to continue in their absence. Taking a long vacation is one way to test the coverage plan and system documentation without suffering bodily harm. You want to discover the gaps in coverage when you are away for a week or two on vacation so that you can fix them when you return.

- Take a break. Breathe. Nobody's last words were ever "I wish I had spent more time at the office." Relax—it's only 1s and 0s.

## CHAPTER 10

Email Management

How we manage our email says a lot about how we manage our time. Most system administrators let email manage them, not the other way around. This chapter discusses dos and don'ts for managing email. I propose a better way to manage email, how to deal with the backlog you may currently have, and other email-related issues.

USER FRIENDLY by Illiad

Managing Your Email

Your email reader is not the most effective time-management tool. Anyone who has tried to use his inbox as his to do list quickly discovers this. It works great for a day or two, then suddenly you get a flood of emails, and it all goes to hell in a handbasket. Messages are mixed with to do items, and there is no way to prioritize or keep track of things.

Therefore, my recommendation is to keep your inbox clean.

To keep your inbox clean, you need to have a plan for what you're going to do with every email message you receive. Each possibility has to end with "delete the message," or your inbox will start to fill up. In fact, if you don't delete it soon, you'll be stuck going back over old messages to figure out what to do with them. That means you'll read each email message twice (maybe more) before acting on it—not very efficient.

When dealing with interruptions in Chapter 2, we used a system called delegate, record, do. For dealing with email, we have a few more options:

- Filter
- Delete unread
- Read and...
  - Delete
  - File
  - Reply, then delete
  - Delegate or forward, then delete
- Do now, then delete

I know to an experienced email user like you these points seem obvious and self-explanatory, but indulge me. You might know how to manage email, but are you really doing it? The following sections go into more detail and include tips I've picked up along the way.

Filter

Email filters are a big part of my email management. By having email automatically filtered based on content, subject, or whom the email is from, I can set up routines.

The bulk of my email comes from email lists that I subscribe to. I create a folder for each mailing list I'm on and set up automatic filters to file messages from each mailing list to their appropriate folder.

I group the folders into two parent folders or groups. The first group is the folders (mailing lists) I read every day. To me, this is like reading the daily newspaper. I try to keep this group small—small enough that I can read all the messages that accumulate each day in 15 minutes.

The other group of folders is for my less-important mailing lists. For these, if I haven't gotten around to reading the folder by Friday, I empty the entire folder without reading any of the contents. This prevents me from accumulating megabytes of outdated messages. I delete with confidence: if it was really important, I would have seen it elsewhere, too.

I also have one unofficial group of mailing lists. These are the lists that receive messages so rarely that it doesn't make sense to set up a filter for them. They might as well go to my inbox directly. An example of this is the list that announces new releases of the Unix sendmail program. The announcements are rare enough that it's OK to let them go to my inbox, and setting up a filter would be more work than it is worth. Managing a lot of usually empty folders would be a pain.

I have another rule about email lists. Once a month I evaluate the lists I'm subscribed to and unsubscribe from one of them. This is a routine (see Chapter 6) that I schedule for the first of each month. Some months this is easy: I've joined a list that turned out not to be very useful. Other months it's not so easy, but I do it anyway. Otherwise, I'm going to end up on every email list on the planet. This is similar to what some people do to keep their closets organized: when they buy new clothes, they get rid of an equal number of old clothes. Here's a mantra for you:

> If you aren't sure if an email list is useful, it isn't.

Delete Unread

The next category of email messages are the ones that I can delete without reading. These are usually maintenance announcements from the building supervisor, spam, or other "blast" email that I know has little relevance to my life.

When I was at Bell Labs, I would often receive a printed announcement in my office mailbox telling me that construction would be blocking a particular entrance. I would also receive email about this, often multiple times. Of course, if I was driving anywhere near that entrance, I would see tons of construction and signs notifying me to turn back. Eventually, I realized that unless the message mentioned something that affected computers (power, cooling, etc.), I could delete those messages without reading them.

Read and...

Email that we read has to be processed somehow. My goal is to touch each email only once. By *touch*, I mean deal with it and send it to its final resting place. If I don't have time to read a message, I let it sit unread. I've found that when I choose to leave a partially read email in my mailbox to finish reading later, I always end up reading the whole thing again. Thus, I'm reading at least part of it twice, which isn't very efficient. So, I've created a rule for myself: if I start to read a message, I have to finish it and then act upon it using one of the methods listed here.

Server-Side Email Filtering

I prefer to do my email filtering on the server side. That usually requires using an IMAP-based system or prohibits the use of a POP-based system. While most email clients nowadays will filter messages as they arrive, filtering them on the server has some significant benefits.

First of all, I use a variety of email clients on many different machines. I can't be expected to keep the filters in sync on all of the machines. IMAP handles that well.

Second, the filters I can do on a server are done at arrival time, not when I run the client. In other words, the filters trigger even when I'm not around or I don't have my email client running. That means I can construct filters that do things such as send a copy to your pager or cell phone or run a command to process the message.

At one company I worked for, the secretaries would email everyone in the entire building when there was leftover food after a sales presentation. I would often miss these announcements because I was in the machine room. That was, of course, until I set up server-side filtering. Any email with a subject line containing "lunch" or "food" would be copied to my pager (this was before cell phones). Often, I would get to the food before anyone else.

Now I also receive copies on my cell phone that mention lunch, food, dinner, the word "urgent," or anything that comes from my boss, my boss's boss, my significant other, and a few other important people. It not only helps me focus (I'm not checking my email all the time), but it helps me not miss the really important emails.

If your email server permits you to reach a Unix/Linux command line, there is a good chance you can use *procmail* (*http://www.procmail.org*) for your server-side filtering. I'm such a fan of procmail that I often tell people, "If you aren't using procmail, you're working too hard."

Some IMAP4-based email servers have server-side filtering using something called Sieve. Made popular with the Cyrus IMAP server for Unix/Linux, Sieve is an open standard for server-side filtering. That means that any client can be used to update the filters on any server that conforms to IETF RFC 3028 (*http://www.ietf.org/rfc/rfc3028.txt*). The home page for Sieve is *http://www.cyrusoft.com/sieve/*.

Delete

We all have messages that we can read and delete right away. These are the messages that require no action from us. Items that I'm cced on often fall into this category, as do emails that just acknowledge that someone received an email that I sent.

I receive a lot of automated messages from various systems. Request Tracker from Best Practical bccs me on any changes to requests in certain categories or queues. This lets me keep tabs on what's going on. Unless I need to chime in, I can read and delete these.

File

I try not to file a lot of email. I know many people who file every message they receive. They have 500 folders and spend a few minutes deciding the perfect folder for each message. I prefer, "When in doubt, throw it out." If I discover that I need that information a few days later, I can find it in my trash folder. If I need it much later, I can go to the original source or find some poor fool who spends his time meticulously filing every message he receives.

Some people set up a filter to save a copy of every incoming email message (excluding those from mailing lists) to an archive folder. Then they are confident that they can delete any message without fretting. If they later discover that they shouldn't have deleted something, they can go to the archive. I believe that as disk space becomes cheaper, this will become more popular. Someday email will include special features to handle this better.

 There are legal implications to archiving all email. Check your corporate email retention policy.

The email that I do save goes into one of two folders: Save and Receipts. If it is something documenting a financial exchange, I put it in the Receipts folder. Otherwise, it goes in my Save folder. I used to have a million little folders, one for every occasion. It turns out that scrolling through all those folders was more time than it was worth. If I need it, it's in Save or Receipts.

Reply, then delete

Email that requires a reply should get a reply right away so that people aren't kept waiting.

The Feathers Email Folder

Besides Save and Receipts, I have one other folder called Feathers.

When someone compliments me, it is a "feather in my cap." Therefore, any time I get a thank-you email or anything complimentary, I move the message to this folder. When I'm having a depressing day, I flip though these messages to cheer myself up.

This folder is also useful when I have to write my yearly performance review.

The problem is that sometimes the reply will require a lot of work, and I won't have time for it right then. In that case, I put the email into my to do list management system so that it won't be lost, but I can still delete it from my inbox.

For example, my reply is usually, "I've added this to the to do list. I'll get back to you with a full answer by [insert date]." I then forward the email to our request-tracking system.

With a system like RT from Best Practical (*http://bestpractical.com*), you can do this in one step. Simply forward the entire message (attachments and all) to the person and bcc the email address that creates new RT tickets. Add a message to the top saying, "Hi! I got your message. I should get back to you by [insert date] with an answer."

No muss, no fuss.

Sometimes it's more appropriate to record the request in your organizer and send email to the person when you expect to have an answer.

Either way, the message is recorded and no longer needs to be in your inbox.

(If you don't have a request-tracking system, I highly recommend you make it a top priority to install one. Some of the best ones are free, including the aforementioned RT.)

I used to think it was polite to reply to every email I received. Polite? I thought it was my duty! Now I actually reply to very little email. If someone sent me a joke, I don't reply with, "Thanks, it was hilarious" or the more annoying, "Gosh, I've been on that interweb since 1987 and I've seen that a million times." I just delete it and move on.

Unless, of course, the email asks for a specific reply. Then I forward it back to the person with a quick answer. By including the entire message, I don't have to explain context. Life is too short to write long memos.

Delegate or forward, then delete

Some email requires delegating a task to someone else. I always cc the person who made the request so she knows who it has been delegated to. Sometimes I create a to do item in my organizer to follow up on the item on a particular day, which helps me stay in the loop and verify that the task wasn't dropped.

Sometimes forwarded email—messages to my boss or my team to keep them updated—doesn't require follow up. I also don't reply to emails spreading the latest hilarious Internet joke—such as when I learned about a seven-year-old boy in England, named Craig Shergold, trying to get into the *Guinness Book of World Records* by amassing the largest postcard collection. Oh, wait, that's an urban legend.

Do Now, Then Delete

Requests that are important or quick to execute should be done now. Usually these are requests from the boss or simple requests that would take less time to do than to submit into a request-tracking system or organizer. If something takes less than two minutes to complete, it is less work to do it now than to spend time recording it to do later.

Jump Starting the Process

The difficult part about this system can be getting started. If you have 2,000 email messages in your inbox, this system must sound like some kind of unrealistic fantasy.

My recommendation? Forget the really old stuff and move forward.

Some mail clients have special archive functions. However, it is just as easy to create a folder called "DeadItems-2005-11-19" (or whatever the date is) and move all items older than that date into that folder.

Now you have a clean inbox, and if someone does need you to pull something out of your old archive, it's all right there.

And if you don't touch that folder for a full year, burn it onto a CD-ROM, delete it, whatever, just get it out of your mailbox. If you haven't touched it for a year, there is little chance you'll touch it ever. Your email client will run faster now that it doesn't have to manage such a huge index.

I'm still waiting for someone to write a program that will seek out all email older than a year and burn them onto a CD-ROM, along with a little Java program that would let me search and browse the messages, and even restore selected items to my mail reader. Alas, such a beast doesn't exist. I even have a cool name for the technique: "Pickled Email" (like the food-preserving process). If you invent such a tool, you are free to use that name—no charge.

Does it sound impossible to just let go of 2,000 email messages?

Let me ask you this: when are those 2,000 email messages actually going to get processed?

Next month?

How long have you been saying "next month"?

Before I developed the previously described technique, I tried two other methods unsuccessfully:

- **Random 100 a day.** I used to think that if every day I could process and delete 100 old messages, I could clean out my inbox in a month. However, when I tried to do that, my inbox just got bigger! I couldn't keep it up for a full month. Plus, processing 100 messages can take more than an hour. That's 20 to 30 hours—more than half a week—to complete this project. I could do other things with that time.

- **By person.** Another technique that I tried was to process my inbox by person. I'd deal with all the messages from a particular person. They'd get a flood of mail: "Do you still need this?" "What about this?" "Hey, I finally read this, it was hilarious. Thanks!" Then I was done with that person forever...or until the next time I got behind in reading email.

Though the by-person technique also failed for me, it did have a benefit over processing 100 messages a day: it let me set priorities. I could pick the more important people in my life rather than a smattering of messages from random people.

However, realistically, once you have more than 1,000 or so messages in your inbox, I think you have to accept that those messages are never going to really get processed.

Sorry, they just aren't.

I know it's difficult to accept because it was difficult for me, too. However, one day I looked at the oldest messages in that big pile and realized that some of them were more than five years old—from another era.

If you reply to an email that is that old, people often think you are crazy, or they question if your reply was caught in a stuck queue, or they make a joke about time travel.

What's the worst that could happen? If the email was truly urgent, you would have already received another request, or you would have gotten in trouble. Huge inboxes are full of messages that are, essentially, dead.

So, if they are never going to get processed, why not move them to an archive and forget about them? Your mail client will work faster without all those messages eating up memory and other resources. It will start up faster, too.

Summary

- Most system administrators receive more email than they know what to do with. If you don't manage your email, email will manage you. Get control over your email and you'll be a long way toward regaining control over your time.
- Your inbox is a lousy way to manage your to do list.
- The goal is to get to an empty inbox. To do that, all actions you take on an email must end with either deleting or filing the message. To that end, I recommend a project that involves handling each message in one of these ways: filter, delete unread, read and process, or do and delete.
  - **Filter.** Use filtering software to pre-process your email and automate many tasks.
  - **Delete unread.** Certain kinds of messages can be deleted safely without reading.
  - **Read and process.** Whether the email needs to be read, forwarded, recorded in an organizer or request tracker, or filed, make sure you complete the task and remove it from your Inbox. Don't let it linger.
  - **Do and delete.** If a task can be done in a few minutes, do it now then delete the message.
- To deal with the backlog you may have accumulated until now, I recommend that you save it somewhere and forget about it. If a message was really important, someone would have come after you. Email is ephemeral. The older a message gets, the less value it has.

## CHAPTER 11

Eliminating Time Wasters

This chapter helps you identify time wasters and explores ways to eliminate them.

Let me tell you a little about myself. I love reading Usenet newsgroups (Net-News). I can read bulletin boards for hours. Before the Web existed, Usenet was where I spent most of my online time. I would have been an A student if it hadn't been for Usenet. Darn Usenet!

In my defense, I was quite good at reading Usenet. I tried every new release of every NewsReader on an eternal quest for the one that would enable me to read the most articles in the shortest amount of time. I actually did benchmarks.

I could whip through articles like you wouldn't believe. Seriously—other Usenet aficionados would watch me and ask for tips.

Then one day I came up with the most amazing optimization to the process. I decided to stop reading Usenet all together. I gained a couple of hours each day.

The ultimate process improvement is to eliminate the process. Eliminate, don't automate. (But if you must automate, read Chapter 13.)

The problem is identifying what is worthwhile and what is worth eliminating.

What Is a Time Waster?

I define a *time waster* as any activity that has a low ratio of benefit to time spent.

Everything has some kind of benefit. Spending five hours playing video games has an entertainment benefit. However, other things have benefits that might be more valuable to you. For example, spending the same

amount of time to increase your quality of living by doing home repairs has longer-lasting benefits than blasting millions of pixilated aliens.

The things that waste our time at work are different—phone calls with people who never stop talking, inefficient processes, waiting around for all our lunch buddies to assemble so we can leave for lunch, etc.

Avoiding the Tempting Time Wasters

Some time wasters are just irresistible. It comes down to "everything in moderation." Short conversations around the watercooler break up the boredom and monotony of the workday and let us return to work refreshed. Multihour conversations about nonwork topics, on the other hand, are not so valuable.

The problem is that it is difficult to do things in moderation. As Oscar Wilde said, "I can resist everything but temptation." It's difficult to say to yourself, "I'll just play video games for a minute" or "I'll just look at the subject lines of my email and only read the important ones." Soon you're deleting spam, replying to requests, and then you look at your clock and see that a few hours have passed.

So what works?

I can avoid temptation if I set up rules of thumb and mantras for myself (see Chapter 3) and then find ways to enforce them.

It would be nice if every five minutes our brains would think, "Gosh, what's the benefit of what I'm doing right now?" That would help us recognize when we've fallen into a time waster and snap out of it. Sadly, we're not built that way.

I've found that it's better to set up rules for myself. Rules such as "When this alarm goes off, I'm going to stop playing this game." At home, I have an old-fashioned kitchen timer with a loud bell that requires two hands to turn off (one to hold the device, the other to turn a knob to 0). Thus, I can't just slap an off button and return to my video game. (I also enjoy the irony of being surrounded by technology but using an antique timer.)

In the office, I'd feel silly with the mechanical timer going off all the time, and the noise would disturb my coworkers. Therefore, I use other alarms and reminders, such as iCal.

> Rule of thumb: set an alarm before doing something "just for a minute."

While I find that I can be much more productive in an office with the door closed (due to the lack of interruptions and noise), there are times when having a coworker with me makes it easier to avoid temptation.

> Nothing makes it easier to resist temptation than a proper bringing-up, a sound set of values—and witnesses.
>
> —Franklin P. Jones

Working with someone on a project can make it easier to stay focused. First of all, if I am interrupted, I have the excuse, "Sorry, I'm working with someone right now. Can you come back later?" However, the bigger reason it works is that I just don't even think about the temptations. For example, I can't check my other email inbox, the one I use for personal stuff, right in front of my coworker.

Common Time Wasters

Here are some common work time wasters and advice about how to better manage them.

- **Junk items in your to do list.** Everyone's to do list has a few junk items. Show your to do list to your manager and see if she faints. Maybe she'll eliminate some items, maybe she'll even take responsibility for speaking to the person who made the request. There may be routine (repeated) items on your list that your manager didn't know about. Once, I showed my to do list to my manager, and he saw that every morning I scheduled 15 minutes a day to manually check and fix a problem we'd been having. Ah, finally he saw the value in getting that system replaced!

- **Too many email lists.** How many mailing lists are you on—10, 20, 100? I remove myself from one email list each month. It's a repeating item on my first-of-the-month to do list. I find that during the course of the month I subscribe to email lists that look interesting. If I don't remove myself from lists every so often, I'll eventually be on every list on the planet. (See Chapter 10 for more email tips.)

- **Bulletin boards, Usenet, etc.** The signal-to-noise ratio is so low on most bulletin boards that they rarely have much work-related value.

- **Chat systems.** While I recognize that many people use IRC and Instant Message systems for work-related tasks, nonwork use of chat systems seems to have very little benefit, especially during work hours.

- **The office "drop by."** I find that people are more likely to drop by and chat if my desk faces the door. Turn your chair so people can't catch your eye from the hallway.

- **Salespeople and recruiters.** I used to find it terribly difficult to get off the phone with salespeople and recruiters who would call me. I found the secret was to say, "Thank you, I'm not interested," and hang up. Only once in 10 years did I accidentally hang up on someone whom I shouldn't have. He called back.

- **Manual processes.** There are many programming languages that are geared toward making it easy for system administrators to automate their tasks. Perl is the most popular. Python and Ruby are growing in popularity. Look for a book on that programming language at your local computer bookstore. The O'Reilly *Cookbook* series is also extremely helpful for automating tasks. More on the topic of automating processes in Chapter 13.

Office Socializing

Technical people, contrary to popular stereotype, can be very social people. There are certainly business benefits to the bonding and networking that comes from standing around the watercooler, talking with coworkers. However, there are limits.

Once, I had a coworker who liked to talk about politics and could spend an entire afternoon pontificating (he didn't let others talk much) about current events. The benefit of participating in these conversations was very little, and yet they would draw many people out of their cubicles. I disagreed with him, nearly always, so I was often drawn in because I didn't want his opinions to go unchallenged. In fact, I think those who disagreed with him were more tempted to stop working and join in the debates.

Alas, these conversations were one big waste of time. I couldn't even claim that these sessions had some kind of team-building benefit as his beliefs were very disturbing and off-putting at times. I couldn't put an end to them—I wasn't his manager, and no manager seemed to find a problem with what was going on—but at least I didn't have to get sucked in. Thus, I learned to detect this situation and either bring the discussion back to something work related or to quietly go back to my desk.

Think about all the time that you have spent talking with coworkers about *The Lord of The Rings*; the newest comic book to be turned into a movie; which is better—Emacs or vi, Windows or Linux; or whatever else we geeks talk about. Were any of these discussions valuable? Sure, if you have a light amount of work, there is value to social discussions. But when they carry on for more than an hour?

I believe that most people don't even realize how much time they spend on this habit. Make a point of timing the next marathon conversation about why *Babylon 5* was better than *Star Trek*. You'll be surprised at how difficult it can be to detect when you're in such a conversation and equally surprised at how long the conversation can be.

Be conscious of these conversations. Get good at detecting when they have gone from quick discussion to time waster, and walk away.

Wasteful Meetings

We can often find ourselves deluged with meeting after meeting. That's OK if work is getting done, but learn how to detect when meetings are wasteful.

There are many kinds of meetings, but let's group them into two general types: status meetings and work meetings. *Status meetings* are just that: people reporting on progress on their aspects of a project. *Work meetings* are when people try to get work done.

It can be a waste of everyone's time if you try to problem-solve during a status meeting. If something can't be resolved quickly, pick a time for the involved parties to work it out—don't waste everyone's time. I find it useful to have that meeting immediately after the current meeting. People not involved can leave or drop off the conference call. Everyone is already together, so there's usually no scheduling conflicts to work out.

When I email an announcement of a meeting, I indicate whether it is a work or status meeting. This makes it clear what people should expect and puts them in the right mindset. It also makes it easier for the facilitator to cut off inappropriate discussions when they arise.

As a participant, I realized that I had an influence on whether the meeting was going to be a waste of time. Being on time significantly improved the meeting's efficiency. Being prepared (reading the material being reviewed, etc.) meant I wasn't dragging the meeting down. If I was presenting material, emailing copies to everyone a day early made other people better prepared (though that meant I had to be prepared a day early). I always send an email reminder about meetings 24 hours in advance. This reduces the number of people who arrive late or people who disrupt the meeting's effectiveness by not showing up at all.

Tips for Meeting Facilitators

- Always send a reminder email 24 hours in advance.
- Make it clear whether this is a status or work meeting.
- List the full date ("Friday, Dec 2," not just "tomorrow").
- List the time. If you work across time zones, list the time and time zone; don't assume people know your time zone. Better yet, include the time converted to all appropriate zones.
- Include URLs to the documents people will need. Even if this is the third meeting about a particular document, keep including the URL. (Include the document as an attachment only when you have no other choice or when some members don't have access to your Wiki.)
- Include a written agenda—a simple outline of the issues to be covered.
- Show up five minutes early, or earlier if there is audio/visual equipment to be set up.
- If you want people to show up on time, don't announce that the meeting starts at 2 p.m., announce that it starts at 1:54 p.m. People will show up to find out why it starts at such a strange time.
- Always start on time. If people are constantly late, start on time and put the most important items first. Don't repeat the items for latecomers; tell them the info will be in the minutes. People will start coming on time. (They'll hate you, but they'll be on time.)

I learned to hold back from having side conversations. I realized that while I felt my witty comments were a gift to all who heard them, they derailed meetings more than I had realized; so, I learned to keep my mouth shut.

As WiFi technology became more pervasive, I found that I could IM my witty comments to just a friend or two, which satisfied my need to be heard without causing too much distraction. Finally, for meetings that were a complete waste of my time, but unavoidable, I could bring a laptop and get work done, keeping an ear open for the important bits. However, I did find that when I was doing this, it was polite to sit in a less visible spot, and it was OK to do this only if there was a large crowd of people.

Of course, work isn't the only place where we waste time.

Standing Around a Video Store Deciding What to Rent

Ever spend an hour walking around a video store trying to figure out what you want to rent? Do friends and coworkers often mention movies that sound great, but once you walk into the store you can't remember any of them? It happens to all of us.

There is a solution.

In your organizer, keep a list of movies that people mention. PDA users can create a note called "Videos." PAA users can put a sheet of paper under "V" in the A–Z notes section. Any time someone mentions a movie that you'd like to see, write it down.

Now when you enter a video store, open to that list and rent the first thing on the list. You'll spend more time watching movies and less time trying to remember their names.

Alternatively, there is a service called Netflix (*http://netflix.com*) that lets you rent DVDs by mail. Their web site lets you maintain a queue of movies you'd like to see. When you return a DVD, they immediately mail you the first available DVD on your list. Now, when a coworker mentions a great movie, you can log into the Netflix web site and add it to your queue. You can even add films that haven't been released yet. They'll float to the top of the list and you'll get them when they are released. That's perfect for all those "wait until it's out on video" recommendations.

The web site lets you rearrange the items on your queue. There are utilities for Windows and Mac that let you manipulate your list a little easier than you can from the Netflix web site—Netflix Freak for Mac OS X is very popular.

Watching Less Bad TV

Let me make one thing clear: I love TV. I'm not one of those elitists who goes around proudly announcing that they don't watch, nay, don't even own a TV. I think TV is great. In the last 15 years, it has gone from being a total wasteland to a wasteland filled with pearls. The problem is keeping the pearls and avoiding the waste.

From a time management perspective, the problem with TV is that it expects us to schedule our lives around when shows are broadcast, not when we want to watch a particular show.

As a result, when we do turn on the TV, we don't watch what we want to watch, we watch the best show that happens to be on at that moment. Very inefficient.

Then came DVRs. They enable you to record shows to a hard disk and watch them any time you want. There are many brands, but Tivo has the most geek appeal because there's a Linux box under the hood.

I bought my Tivo to help me watch *less* TV, and watch higher-quality shows when I am watching TV. In other words, when I did have time for TV, I wanted the pearls; I didn't want to settle for the best thing on right now.

After using my Tivo for a few months, I found that I was watching more and more TV. I needed to reverse this trend.

That's when I invented Tom's Three Tivo Rules to help me watch less TV:

Rule 1

> If you watch all the way to the end of the program, you have to delete it. Don't give me any of that "Oh, I'll want to watch that again" logic. You don't have enough time to watch everything that gets recorded, let alone watch it a second time.

Rule 2

> If you add anything to the list of shows that are automatically recorded (Season Passes), you have to delete something of equal length and frequency. Alternative: each month you have to delete at least one hour worth of Season Passes.

Rule 3

> If it's about to get old enough to be automatically deleted, let it expire. No extending the date. Archiving it to tape because "I'll find time to watch it later" isn't allowed (see Rule 1 about how much free time you have). Dude, ya just gotta learn to let it go. For me, the only exceptions to this rule are the three shows at the top of my list. I practically bought my Tivo so that I'd never miss these programs: *The Daily Show*, *The West Wing*, and *24*.

These are my personal rules. They were devised to help me use Tivo to reduce the amount of TV that I watch. Your mileage may vary.

Laundry and Housecleaning

Housework can take a lot of time. If you do not have laundry facilities where you live, spending a couple hours each week at a laundromat can be significant, especially if you have very little free time outside work. I'm a fan of "by the pound" laundry services. In my neighborhood, there are two places that will wash and fold my clothes for 85 cents per pound. Rather than killing half a day each week, I spend a few minutes dropping off my clothes on the way to work, and I pick them up on the way home or the next day.

It costs me about $20 per week. While $80 each month sounds like a lot of money, it starts to make sense when it frees up time that I can spend socially, doing activism, or writing this book. It's worth it.

Housework is another drag on one's time. A visit from a cleaning service once or twice a month can save a lot of time and make your place more presentable. Typical service includes vacuuming all carpets and floors, washing the kitchen floor, dusting all surfaces, and cleaning all bathrooms from top to bottom.

A clean house has many benefits. It's easier to host social events if you have a clean house. People are more willing to show up if your home isn't a disaster area. The time you save by having a cleaning service can be used to host more social nights at your place. Despite the modern convenience of staying in touch with friends via Instant Messenger, having friends over to hang out is highly valuable and builds stronger friendships than IM can. It's also cheaper than a night out, which can offset the cost of the cleaning.

An unexpected benefit you will discover is that a cleaning service forces you to clean up and straighten your messes the day before the service arrives. The precleaning twice a month keeps my personal clutter in check.

A cleaning service is most economical when the cost is divided by a few people. If you share a house with others, having a cleaning service every other week can be a godsend, and it helps to avoid arguments about whose turn it is to clean. Plus, I can't imagine four typical male system administrators sharing a house and it not looking like a disaster area and smelling like a locker room. This fixes many problems.

Hardware/Software Installation

Speaking of paying people to do work for you, when I have the budget, I find it useful to pay for installation of the hardware/software that we buy at work. This is particularly important for something that we'll never be repeating.

As an example, let's look at the process of installing a large backup/restore system and tape library. The installation has two parts. First, we do the installation of the hardware and software. This phase ends when we have one server being backed up properly. The second part is the ongoing add-change-delete of systems that are being backed up.

The learning curve for the first part is huge, and yet the payoff is very small. We will spend days, possibly weeks, setting up everything, battling bad manuals and crazy hardware problems. We won't be using this knowledge again because once the system is installed, we won't be installing another one. What might take us weeks could take a VAR or reseller a day or two because they have done it many times. It's their specialty. They know what the pitfalls are and how to avoid them.

The second part has a much better payoff. Learning how to add a new backup server, configure it to back up a new disk, and remove servers or disks has an excellent payoff. It is knowledge gained that we will use time and time again.

Another example is automated OS installation. Setting up a system to automatically load the OS and related applications on a workstation can be complicated, but it has a huge payoff, especially if you reload machines often or purchase many new machines. Examples of this kind of thing include Microsoft RIS, Solaris JumpStart, Red Hat KickStart, and FreeBSD NetBoot. It can be much more cost efficient to pay someone to set up the system and teach you how to make maintenance modifications (adding new software, and so on) rather than struggle through the initial installation alone.

This kind of consulting can be expensive and, therefore, it must be thought of during the budgeting process. Even though installation charges may be 20, 50, or even 100 percent as high as the purchase price of the hardware and software, paying someone to do the initial installation can be well worth it. Especially if this will free you up to work on other projects.

If you do take this advice, remember to shadow the person and have them explain what they are doing as they do it. That way, you get the benefit of his experience and understanding of how the system works, which is useful when you need to debug a problem. It may take some of your time, but not as much as if you try to do the installation yourself.

Others

There are plenty of other time-wasting activities that we can all manage much better. Hopefully the previous list has included a good sampling of work-related and personal time wasters to jog your memory and help you start thinking about the time wasters in your life that you can either manage better or eliminate completely. Of course, what's a waste of time for one person is an important part of life to someone else. Everyone is different.

Strategic Versus Tactical

For a system administrator, the ultimate time waster is any task that could be eliminated if only we had time to build the infrastructure to make such busywork go away. In other words, the ultimate time management technique for a system administrator is a good IT infrastructure.

Strategic tasks are those dealing with long-term planning, like constructing a security policy, getting buy-in from management, and deploying the policy. Tactical tasks are specific tasks related to a particular process, such as formatting a hard drive or installing a new PC.

The problem is that we get so caught up with tactical tasks that we never feel that we have time for strategic work. We're so busy mopping the floor that we don't have time to fix the leaking faucet.

You won't need to spend time handing out IP addresses if you deploy a DHCP server. You won't find yourself spending days fixing security problems if you have a modern and pervasive security program with things like automatically updating virus/malware/spam detection, self-defending networks, and policies that are supported by the highest levels of management. You won't spend afternoons debugging oddball Windows problems that turn out to be slight misconfigurations if you have an infrastructure that automates operating system installation so that every new machine starts out right. You won't spend nights restoring data from backup tapes if you have a server infrastructure that includes proper power, cooling, and redundant storage (RAID). (Not that RAID replaces the need for disaster recovery backups.)

The key is to make time for the strategic projects. Get them onto your calendar and schedule time for the individual steps in your to do list. My rule is to always have one strategic project going on. I'd like to have 50, but if I spread myself too thin, I won't get any of them done. It's better to pick one good project that gets done than to start 50 that never get finished. The advice in the section "Prioritization for Impact" in Chapter 8 will help you narrow down the project. Get consensus on which project will have the biggest impact, and get the whole team working on it until it's complete.

If you are looking for a good book on this topic, I recommend *The Practice of System and Network Administration*. It's more than 700 pages and very complete. I am, however, a little biased.

Summary

- A time waster is any activity that has a low ratio of benefit to time spent. Rather than trying to do these activities more efficiently, it is better to try to eliminate them.

- Certain activities can expand to fill all your time. You can snap out of it by setting a time limit. Make self-imposed rules such as, "When I start to do [insert activity], I will set an alarm to remind me to stop 10 minutes from now."

- Nothing makes it easier to resist temptation than a witness. Sharing an office with a coworker can eliminate any inclination to do nonwork activities while you're at work.

- There are many time wasters in modern life: junk items on the to do list, email lists, chatrooms, nonwork discussions at work, unwanted salespeople and recruiters, manual processes that could be automated, and so on. Once identified, they can be eliminated.

- At home, you can manage time wasters better by using a digital video recorder to manage your TV, "videos to rent" lists and Netflix so you spend less time wandering around video stores, and laundry and housecleaning services so you have more free time for fun.

- Learning to install something that will only be installed once has limited payback. For complicated installations like centralized backup/restore systems, budgeting to have installation done by the vendor or VAR can be a significant win.

- For a system administrator, the ultimate time waster is any task that could be eliminated if only you had time to build the infrastructure to make such busywork go away. In other words, the ultimate time management technique for a system administrator is a good IT infrastructure. By thinking strategically, you can eliminate tactical tasks over the long term. In other words, you can stop mopping the floor and fix the leaking faucet.

## CHAPTER 12

Documentation

This chapter is about how a good documentation repository can help us as system administrators, especially in our effort to manage our time better.

But first, let's talk about why we dislike, fear, and generally avoid writing documentation.

We're suspicious of anyone who asks us to document what we do because it sounds like the precursor to being fired. If we document what we do, we can be replaced. Alternatively, the request to have everything documented comes from outside our group, usually from someone who has gotten "ISO 9001 fever" and doesn't realize that documenting processes is a means to an end, not the other way around.

It can be very difficult to start writing a document. "Documentation" summons an intimidating image of a 1,000-page book describing everything we do, how it's done, and how things work. Where the heck would we start if we had to write that?

System administrators are often perfectionists. We could never document *everything*. Why start a project if it can't be finished? Because of the time it takes to write, documentation often becomes outdated during the writing. Why write something that will be useless the day it is completed?

Besides, there is always a line of people outside our offices requesting that we do urgent things. That's always going to trump documenting. Writing requires long stretches of uninterrupted time. No system administrator has that, right?

Lastly, geeks hate printed documents. Why kill a tree?

This chapter proposes something so different that I hate to call it documentation. Instead, we're going to make an information repository that is accessible, updatable, and useful. Best of all, it will serve our time management needs.

Document What Matters to You

In place of big ol' scary documentation, what do system administrators need? You need repositories to store the information that will help you from a time management perspective. Your boss may have her reasons for wanting you to maintain documentation, but I recommend that your inspiration be something different—selfish. Build documentation repositories that serve you and your time management needs, not the seemingly irrelevant needs of your boss or quality department. Specifically, SAs need two repositories:

- **Customer-facing repository.** Documents that you want users of your network to have access to, such as the policies and procedures they should follow to get service.
- **Internal IT repository.** The info you need internally to help you do your job, such as contact info for vendors, written instructions for tasks, and so on.

The first repository saves you time by making customers more self-sufficient. It deflects them away from bothering you. Why should they call you to ask a question when they could read about it? This way, they will only call you when they need clarification. Many customers prefer the self-help route simply because it saves them from embarrassment when they ask silly questions.

The second repository is useful because you make it useful. In particular, you record all the processes, procedures, and reference materials that *you* need at your fingertips. It is another opportunity to store something digitally so that it doesn't take up space in your brain. It reduces the work your brain has to do so that you can be more focused. Focus is good.

I suggest two repositories because one needs to be freely accessible by all customers, while the other may contain sensitive information that should be restricted for security reasons.

In these two repositories, you should accumulate:

- How customers can request service or get help (possibly a simple decision tree)
- A single place to find all your written policies (with links to HR and Legal's equivalent pages)
- A list of vendors and their contacts, along with maintenance contact information
- A list of procedures of the things you have to do a lot or want someone else to be able to do
- A simple network diagram that someone joining your group (or helping out for the day) can use as a reference

You will put this information on a web site with a public area and a private area. To make it easy to start, I'll include a template for each repository. To make it easy to update, I recommend that you use a Wiki. If you're not familiar with Wikis, I describe them in detail in the upcoming section "Wiki Technology." For now, just remember that a Wiki is a web site that is very easy to update.

You can eliminate the fear of the repository never being done by declaring it to be a *living document*. Rather than something that has to be reprinted every time you make a change, you simply maintain the repository on the intranet. You'll update it any time you need to update it. "Done" doesn't mean it's complete and ready to print, it just means that the initial repository has been birthed and is ready to grow.

The Customer-Facing Repository

The first web site is publicly readable, and it contains IT customer documentation.

When a customer browses to your document repository, the main page should be very simple. Here's a template. Create a home page with the following headings:

How to get help
Include a few ways in a bulleted list.

How to request new services
List a few services that someone might need activated and provide a list or link for how she gets started. Some examples might be VPN access and how to request an external web space.

Policies
A bulleted list of links to the policies that you do have written, plus links to any equivalent pages for HR or Legal.

A single place to find all your written policies
   With links to HR and the Legal department's equivalent pages.

This template should be sufficient for any small system administration group that doesn't have a similar web site yet. If you are an IT or CIO organization so large that you laugh at my little template, you probably have a huge home page/web site already and don't need such a template anyway. However, I'm surprised at how many CIO organizations have web sites that are missing at least one of the above items. I also find that large organizations are made up of smaller teams, each of which can benefit from its own repository.

IT policies are the rules by which users of your computers/networks live. These include security policies, service level agreements, acceptable use policies, ethics guidelines, privileged information/access guidelines, and so on. Under IT Policies, link to each written policy that you already have, whether these policies are in HTML, Word, or PDF format. If you don't have any policies, don't include this heading just yet. However, add any of the policies you think you should have to your to do list. If you are looking for inspiration on what policies to add or how to write them, read Chapter 7 (Security) and Chapter 9 (Ethics) of *The Practice of System and Network Administration*. I recommend starting with an acceptable use policy. If your legal department or HR maintains relevant policies, link to them. If these sections do nothing but highlight what policies you are missing, that's a good thing.

This template is only a start. Over time, you will realize things to add or changes to make.

If you have the time and resources, the next step is to improve this home page so that people will want to set it as their default web page. This will encourage people to go to your web site often and use it when they do need, for example, to refer to an IT policy. Add useful things like a Google search box, stock tickers, or company news. Set it as the default page on any new machine you install.

Internal IT Documentation

The second repository contains internal IT documentation: documents that are useful to you and the people on your team. These documents will contain information that is sensitive, and therefore it should be secured in some manner, possibly just by simple password protection. This repository is often a password-protected area of the other repository.

If you don't already have such a repository, here's a template:

- **Vendor contacts and maintenance agreements.** A link to a list of vendors and their contacts, along with maintenance contract information.

- **Internal IT procedures.** A list of procedures you do or want someone else to be able to do. Examples include checklists for setting up new users and cleaning up after departed ones.

- **Network diagrams.** Links to a simple network diagram that someone joining your group (or helping out for the day) can use as a reference. This may be a link to a page of diagrams.

Let's explore each of these a bit more.

Vendor contacts and maintenance agreements

Under Vendor Contacts, create a link to each vendor you deal with. The destination for each link should be a page for that vendor that lists the phone number of your salesperson, the support phone number, and info you will need when you call about a system problem. For example, for one vendor, I list the phone number, the items on their phone menu, and the answers to the questions that I know I'll be asked: the phone number they use to look up my profile, my maintenance contract number, etc. If a vendor has a unique maintenance contract for each piece of equipment I've bought from them, I put all that information in a table. That table also includes a link to the password-recovery procedure for that device, as well as a link to a locally cached copy of that procedure.

You might want to use some kind of server-side include feature to make one page that contains all the other pages. You can print the mega page every so often and keep a copy in your computer room for emergencies. If you're really cool, you'll write a script that will automatically print the document on the first of the month if it has changed since the previous month.

Every time I deal with a vendor, I use this page to contact them, even if the info is also in my personal address book. That way I know the page is up-to-date in the central repository. If I find it has become out-of-date, I update it right then and there.

Internal IT procedures

You'll never list every single procedure for everything you do, and you don't need to. However, my advice is that you document the tricky procedures that you don't do frequently and the procedures that you hate to do.

An example of a tricky procedure is breaking a RAID mirror, then reattaching/rebuilding it. You might "break the mirror" (i.e., detach the main disk from its mirror) before doing an OS upgrade. If the upgrade fails, you can mount the half of the mirror that wasn't upgraded. If the upgrade succeeds, you can reattach and rebuild the mirror. The commands to do all those things are usually relatively tricky. Therefore, the next time you do this kind of thing, create a web page and record the commands that you used and make notes about how you constructed the commands. In the future, you can refer to this page and the whole thing will go faster.

If there are many ways to do something but only one of them is right for your environment, document that specific way (and why it is the right way). Often a HOWTO document found on the Web or as part of a software distribution lists many ways to do something, but you've learned that only one of those is appropriate for your environment. You might want to paste the entire HOWTO document into your repository and add commentary, such as "Use option 3," "Don't do that," or "This shortcut worked on Server B, but do the long version on all other systems." Use color for your comments to make them stand out. Be sure to respect the original document's copyright!

I often create documents that are simply checklists. It's not as intimidating as writing a huge document fully describing every little detail. I don't have a knack for remembering details, so checklists have become a way of life for me. Since the repository is easy to update, other people will contribute to the document over time. It often grows into a full document.

The other procedures you should document are the ones you don't like to do. Sure, it would be nice to document everything you do, but who has the time? Instead, document the processes that you don't like because that creates the materials needed to train someone else to do those processes. I personally hate creating accounts. Even though I've automated the process as much as I can, it's still a pain. Plenty of it can't be automated, especially my checklist of things such as "Visit the customer on his first day to see whether he has any questions" and "Repeat the visit a week later as a follow-up." So I documented the command that I run that creates the account, how I test to make sure the account was created properly, and other things that have to be done when a new employee joins. It isn't *War and Peace*; it isn't even in paragraph form. It's just a bulleted list with some annotations. But now that it's documented, I have a hope of foisting it off on someone else. In Chapter 2, I talked about delegating. A good document repository is an excellent way to make a task easier to delegate.

Heck, that's my general strategy to getting more staff. I document all the tasks that I hate to do, which I would give to an assistant if I had one. The next time there is a hiring opportunity, I can refer to the repository for a list of what to include in the job description for my new assistant: create accounts, change backup tapes, fix common printer problems, and so on. Gosh, isn't it an amazing coincidence that those things are already well-documented and ready for someone else to take over?

Hiring opportunities are rare, but that's OK. I don't need a full-time person. When the development group hires someone to maintain the software build system, there I am with the web page of procedures and tasks that I can foist off onto him. Ain't I a stinker?

Network diagrams

Finally, include your network diagrams. Link to the ones that already exist. If you don't have any, make a simple one to start off, like a WAN diagram or a diagram that shows your LAN and the name of the major servers, and then draw a big cloud that represents all your desktop/laptop hosts. At one job, I found that I repeatedly needed to draw a particular network diagram on a nearby whiteboard to illustrate my point. (The diagram was four dots representing our four sites, the five WAN links that connected them, and an arrow to a cloud representing the Internet connection.) Adding this simple, easy-to-reproduce diagram to the repository was a quick way to get started. In 10 minutes, you should be able to create your first diagram and put it online.

True hot-blooded system administrators probably insist on Visio with photo-realistic server icons and accurate-to-the-millipica placements, but that is a rat hole. Ever start drawing a diagram and suddenly realize you've spent the entire day getting it just right? There's no cheese down that hole. Spend 10 minutes, not 10 hours. I actually prefer to use tools that don't let me do supremely detailed and perfect work so that I'm forced to get the essence of what the diagram should look like and not futz with the details. I often do diagrams with PowerPoint and store the original and PDF copy in the repository.

If you really can't control the desire to draw the perfect diagram, sketch it out on a whiteboard and take a picture with a cheap digital camera; store the picture in the repository. It's fast and it works really well. (If someone complains that they should be redrawn in a more serious drawing package, make sure he has write access to the repository and tell him, "I look forward to your results.")

Also document the important data flows in the company: how does email get in and out of the company, where are your directory servers, and so on.

Wiki Technology

To make a web site (repository) full of pages that are easy to update, use a Wiki. A *Wiki* is a concept, not a particular software package. There are many software packages that give you the Wiki feature. There is the original Wiki (Hawaiian for quick), then there is TWiki, KwikiKwiki, PHPWiki, etc. It's such a good idea that plenty of people have written software systems that give you the feature.

I ignored Wikis because I thought the name was stupid. I thought, "I could never use a system with a goofy name like that, even if it turned lead into gold." I didn't even investigate to find out what a Wiki was. Three years later, I started using a Wiki that someone else had installed and found it extremely helpful to my productivity. Oh, how I regret ignoring Wikis for so long.

So what the heck is a Wiki?

It is a web site in which anyone can edit any page, and linking pages is really easy.

Sounds crazy, right? I mean, if anyone can edit any page, what about vandalism? Someone could come along and delete things, put incorrect information into the system, and so on. It would be a disaster!

I promise you that there are some features that completely eliminate these problems. First, let's just consider the positive side:

- **It's easy to add new pages.** New pages can be added by anyone. If a junior admin is the first to deal with a new vendor, he can add a page for the vendor and start listing contact information and so on.

- **Wikis are centralized and accessible.** Anyone with a web browser can access them (allowing for any access controls in place). No special software is required on the client.

- **Everyone can contribute.** Anyone can edit any page when she sees a typo or has information to add. A document might start as a small checklist, then items are added by someone else, and someone else turns it into a full-blown process document.

- **Wiki pages stay up-to-date.** When anyone can edit any page, you've solved one of the biggest problems with documentation, which is that documents often become out-of-date the moment they are published. Instead, a Wiki is a set of pages that can be updated immediately by the person who spots the dated material.

The problem with document repositories is that there is usually a high barrier to use them. Users have to request an account, be given permission and access, etc.

Wiki Notation and Page Linking

A Wiki lowers the barrier for all of those issues. You don't have to be specially trained to know how to use one—lessons in HTML are not required. You don't need an account to read documents. If you don't have an account when you go to edit a document, you are given the opportunity to create one right then and there. Accounts are created with default permissions that let users do most basic functions. And best of all, while users can write in pure HTML, there is also "Wiki notation," which lets them write plain text that the Wiki formats. For example, Wikis understand that words surrounded by asterisks, underscores, and other symbols are special. If you type ***like this***, it is displayed **like this**. If you type **__like this__** , it is displayed *like this*. If you make a bulleted list by starting a series of lines with *, Wiki transforms those lines into an HTML <ul> bulleted list. Most people pick up these codes very quickly because they use them in email already, and, if they don't, there is plentiful online help explaining the formatting.

Creating links in Wiki is easy, too. If you include a URL, Wiki turns it into a link. However, linking to other Wiki pages is much more fun. Wiki pages have names that are in a special format called a WikiWord. Perl programmers know this as CamelCase or StudlyCaps. It is simply a single word with mixed capitalization. For example, you might name a page ListOfFavoriteThings. Any time you write a sentence on a Wiki page that includes ListOfFavoriteThings, the Wiki turns that word into a link to that page, even if there is no page by that name. In that case, clicking on that link gives the user the opportunity to create a page with that name. In other words, to create a new page, just make a link to it, click on that link, and start editing.

It's also easy to upload documents into a Wiki. The document becomes attached to that page. Therefore, any page can become a document container for PDFs, Microsoft Word documents, and so on. Once, I needed a way for nontechnical people to store Microsoft Word documents. I simply made a Wiki page called TheProjectName and showed them how to upload documents so that the documents were attached to that page. The Wiki displays a table of what files are attached to the page automatically. If a person can't grasp Wiki notation, at the least he can attach documents to a page. A division of labor is created: experts create Wiki pages and structure the repository, less-technical people attach documents to the structure created for them. As those less-technical people get comfortable with Wiki concepts, they make an easy transition to the more technical tasks.

Preventing Wiki Vandalism

There are social controls and technical features in Wikis that combine to make sure vandals and malcontents don't destroy repositories.

First of all, the social controls are quite simple: every change is logged to the person who made the change. You'd be amazed at how effective this is. I estimate that 90 percent of the reason that people don't just go changing things willy-nilly is due to the fact that they're being logged. This is especially true in a corporate environment.

There are also technical features that control vandals. All Wiki pages are kept in a system like RCS, CVS, Subversion, or Microsoft SourceSafe. Thus, there is infinite un-do. You can roll back changes easily, or compare different revisions to a page to see exactly what was changed. Knowing that your vandalism can be undone easily often takes the joy out of the act. If spray paint washed off with the next rainstorm, there would be no joy in writing "Francine loves Harvey" on a nearby overpass.

Most Wikis have access control systems. Each page or set of pages can be restricted as to who can read, write, or rename the page. The default is that anyone can edit the page, thus encouraging "the Wiki way." However, you want your main page, menus, and other pages to be editable only by designated people.

Wiki purists claim that access controls like this aren't needed because the beauty of Wiki culture is that while it is easy for one person to vandalize a page, it is just as easy for someone else to correct the page. That's true, but I sleep better at night knowing that I'm the only person who can edit the page that lists the phone number of my IT department's helpdesk. In Wiki culture, "a Wiki with business features" is code for "a Wiki with access control."

The *coup de grace* against Wiki vandalization is email notification. Most Wiki systems can send email notifications anytime a page is changed. The email usually includes what got changed (an HTML "diff" report) so that you can quickly see if the change was benign or harmful. Some systems default to always notifying the original creator of a page. Some sites configure a Wiki so that any change triggers a notification to the webmaster. I think that's overkill.

While documenting "everything" is a fine goal, never list a password on a web page. Even if the page is password protected and on a secure server, this is just asking for trouble. For example, I once found a site that was supposedly secure because passwords were listed on a page that was only accessible via an SSL connection after entering a password. However, people with shell accounts on the machine could log in and read the file directly. Since this was the main departmental server, everyone had accounts.

The Wiki system that I have the most experience with is called TWiki (*http://www.twiki.org*). Its claim to fame is adding access control. Other systems are available from the ultra simple (one is written in awk) to the extremely full-featured. Some larger systems are including a Wiki as a feature, while some systems are built entirely around the Wiki concept, such as the infinitely fun and amazingly complete open source encyclopedia project, Wikipedia (*http://www.wikipedia.org*).

Summary

- A document repository can be a great time management tool.

    - A repository for customers can give them the information they need so they can bother you less.

    - A repository for internal IT information can help you by creating reference material that saves you time in the future. Checklists can be particularly useful—as are short notes describing how a tricky procedure was successfully done—so that others don't have to reinvent the wheel.

    - A procedure that is sufficiently documented is easier to delegate to someone else. Thus, we can remove a task from our to do list by giving it to someone else.

- Wiki technology removes the entry barrier by making access easy and eliminating the need to learn HTML. By letting anyone edit (nearly) any page, the documents are more likely to be up-to-date.

- Creating a document repository for your IT operation does not need to be intimidating. You can control the scope of the repository by choosing what to document. The templates included in this chapter can help you get started. Wiki technology lets a document grow and evolve over time.

- It can be intimidating to start a new document. Wiki technology makes it easy to create a new document by handling all the linking for you. The initial document can be a simple checklist that will grow over time. You don't need to feel compelled to create the perfect document right from the start. Create something that is useful right now and let it evolve.

A Personal Information Repository

There is some information I want to take everywhere, but it is more than I can fit in a PDA. Certain information doesn't always need instant access, but some kind of access is valuable. Putting it on the Web makes it accessible nearly everywhere, especially with WiFi access being so common. Setting up a password-protected directory is relatively easy.

There is certain information that I keep in a Subversion repository. Subversion, like CVS or Microsoft SourceSafe, lets one access and update a repository of information from anywhere on the network. It's usually used for storing source code and tracking the changes. In theory, wherever I am, I can either download the latest version of the file repository or SSH to a machine that has access already established. I use my repository to store a very large address book and some other notes.

## CHAPTER 13

Automation

Automating our tasks is a special treat. In what other career can we program machines to do our jobs for us? Oh, if only it were that easy. Automating something takes time, but the payback can be enormous.

This chapter doesn't attempt to teach Perl, Python, Ruby, Unix shell, VBasic, or Kix32. Instead, this chapter is about why we automate, what to automate, and how to automate. I'll also include some shortcuts that have helped me through the years.

Automation has the obvious benefit of reducing work for you because the task becomes quicker to do or—through Unix cron or Windows Scheduler—happens automatically without any intervention at all. An unexpected benefit is that an automated task is easier to delegate. Any task you can foist onto someone else is a special victory.

Is It Automated Enough?

Adam Moskowitz, a well-known SA, tells me that his litmus test for whether something is "automated enough" is that he can delegate the task to someone less skilled. For example, once, he automated his company's disk backups to the point that the company secretary was able to take over the daily tape-changing tasks. Each day, the system would send email to her and Adam with the status of the previous night's backup. Usually, the system would simply output instructions about which tapes to change. If there was a failure, she knew not to touch the system until Adam had fixed the problem. Over time, he was able to modify the software to handle more and more failure cases. Soon the system would go months without requiring his intervention.

In this chapter, I will use the terms script and program to mean different things. *Script* implies a short program, possibly only a few lines. A script is usually a BAT file, a few lines of Perl, or a small Unix shell file. I'll use the term *program* when I mean a longer program, one that requires more thought and planning. Programs are usually written with a more formal process that includes requirements gathering, development, and testing. Programs tend to be written in compiled languages like C++ and interpreted languages that are suited to large programs such as Perl, but this is not always the case. Perl programmers, for example, often refer to their code as a Perl script if it is small and a Perl Program if it is large.

What to Automate?

It's difficult to find time to automate processes, so we have to be choosy. We can't automate everything. According to R. A. Lichtensteiger, the problems SAs typically deal with fall into four general categories:

- **Simple things done once.** Category 1 includes most of your daily work. If it is simple and you do it only once, there is no sense in automating it. It would take longer to automate than to do the task.

- **Hard things done once.** Category 2 contains the tasks that are a bit difficult to get right the first time, and by recording the final (working) command into a script, you get a free record of how to do the task next time. If you need to do it once, you'll need to do it again eventually. Things in this category also include multicommand sequences that are best tested one command at a time, building up until you have the entire sequence working. Then you can use the sequence with confidence that it will work.

- **Simple things done often.** Category 3 is the obvious case where automation will pay off with the most impact. The time you invest in automating the procedure will be paid off soon, since the task is one that you perform a lot. Always automate the boring, repetitive stuff.

- **Hard things done often.** Category 4 is where a lot of SAs get stuck because they have bitten off more than they can chew. This is the category where one should look into convincing management to allocate greater resources (time and money) into solving this problem. The result may be the purchase of a commercial product, integration of free and/or open source tools to accomplish the task, or development of an in-house solution.

Now, for the visual thinkers, it may help to see these categories as a chart (Figure 13-1).

	Simple things	Hard things
Done once	Do it manually	Automate it
Done often	Automate it	Buy or write software

Figure 13-1. Categories of SA tasks

People are often surprised to see that I automate simple things done often. If they are simple, why automate at all? I automate a wide variety of processes within Categories 2 and 3, from the biggest tasks to the smallest command lines, for the same reason. Automating tasks gets me repeatability, scalability, and typo-free execution:

- **Repeatability means I can do something consistently many times.** For example, when configuring new machines, I want them all to start out with the same software configuration and preferences. Otherwise, supporting them is going to be a nightmare. If I automate the installation process, then it becomes repeatable, and each machine starts out the same. If I figured out something that works, I want to do it exactly that way every time.

- **Automation can replace the need to memorize something complicated that is done rarely.** Sometimes it just plain takes a long time to figure out the right set of command-line options to get something to work. I turn the single command into a script so that months from now I won't have to reinvent the wheel. That's long-term repeatability. For example, on Mac OS X, I can burn an ISO image onto a CD-ROM with the `hdutil` command. However, rather than reading the manual page each time to help me remember all the different options I like to use, I've encapsulated that one-line command into a script. Even if I don't use that script, I can refer to it to see what combination of options has worked for me.

- **Scalability.** This means that I can do the process no matter how large my network grows. Once I automate a process, I can run the script on all my machines, scaling my knowledge to affect all the hosts on my network. For example, modifying a particular SSH server setting is quite easy for one machine. A few seconds with a text editor, and `sshd_config` is changed. However, if I automate the process, I can then use that procedure on hundreds of machines, possibly letting it run overnight. I don't have to be there for each one. I don't have to care if there are 10 or 10,000 machines being updated.

- **Automation can help replace error-prone procedures.** There are plenty of short procedures that are just plain difficult to type correctly every time. There is a short sequence of commands that I type a lot. In those few lines, I had to repeat a user's login ID (her name) three times and her Unix UID (the number) twice. It's simple to type but easy to make a typo. By turning this task into a script, I prevent the possibility of making a typo. Even though the sequence is only a few lines, it's worth having as a script.

How to Automate

To automate something, first you have to do it manually. Then you write code for each step. Next, you bring the little bits of code together, testing each addition as it is added. Finally, you test the entire system.

Step 1: Do It Manually

The first step to automating a process is to make sure you can do the process manually. Document each step, and make sure you can write code to do that step. Then put all the pieces together.

Many times a protégé has come to me asking for help automating something. "Oh, I've worked on this problem for hours! I'm completely stuck!" he'll say.

"OK," I reply, "show me how you would do this manually."

"I don't know. I can't figure that out."

"The root of your problem is just that, young padawan. Hmmm?"

As discussed in Chapter 12, one of the benefits of documenting a procedure is that writing down the steps is the key to being able to automate something. I wasn't kidding. In fact, when I don't have time to automate something, I write the step-by-step procedure on my Wiki telling someone else how to do the task. When I do that, I've accomplished two things. First, I've contributed to the documentation of how our system works. Second, I've actually performed the first step of automating the process!

 Document the steps, then automate them. If you can't write down the steps, you'll never figure out how to automate them.

The process of writing down the steps forces you to identify all the steps. Unlike keeping all of the steps in your head, you can show the document to other people to have them verify the process.

If you don't have a Wiki, you can use paper and a pencil or a text file. Do the steps manually and record the steps. Any command that you type should be pasted into the text document.

Step 2: Code Each Step

Turn each step into something that can be done from the command line or within a short program. Test each step individually. That is, you might write a series of small scripts, each one verifying that the code you have for that particular step is correct.

If any step involves a graphical user interface (GUI), you must find the command-line equivalents. Some operating systems make this easy. For example, HP-UX's System Administration Manager (SAM) has a button you can press to output the command-line equivalent of the action it is about to perform. Mac OS X has Automator and AppleScript that let you automate processes normally done though the GUI. Windows has many different tools that are similar. However, tools that automate the clicking of buttons may not be as useful as directly setting various registry keys or LDAP entries.

Recommended books for Microsoft Windows administrators:

- *Windows Server Cookbook* (O'Reilly). You can learn a lot from this book by reading it cover to cover. You'll be surprised at how many things you thought could only be done though the GUI that can be scripted easily by a series of registry updates. It will open your mind up to the possibilities. The examples are in many languages, usually VBasic and Perl.

- *Perl for System Administration* (O'Reilly). This book is particularly good if you manage both Unix and Windows systems. It is Perl-centric (obviously) and people with an Enterprise or Unix background may feel more comfortable with it. It is particularly good if you are a big user of Active-Directory and/or LDAP.
- *Win32 Perl Scripting: The Administrator's Handbook* (Sams). This is also a good book, especially if you are new to scripting.

Recommended books for Unix/Linux administrators:

- *Perl for System Administration.* (See the full description under Windows books.)
- *UNIX System Administration Handbook* (Prentice Hall PTR). This book not only teaches the fundamentals of Unix administration, it also includes many valuable resources and tools. Most examples use the command line, which means they can be scripted easily.
- *Essential System Administration* (O'Reilly). Another excellent book that includes many command-line examples.
- *Advanced Bash-Scripting Guide.* Visit *http://www.tldp.org/guides.html*.

Step 3: Bring the Steps Together

Once the code for each step works, you can bring the code for each step together into one big script.

Even when bringing the code together, it is best to add one step at a time. Test after each new step is added. This is called *incremental development* and is the best way to test automation. By testing after each small change, you are more certain that the entire shebang will work when you are done.

For example, when we hire a new person, we have to create his account in the LDAP directory, set up his web space on our internal web server, and test his account to make sure it was created properly. Each of these steps can be automated individually. We verify that we have working commands for each step. Then we put the first set of commands into a script and test just that. We make sure the command-line option-processing junk works, any debugging commands we want work, and so on. We run the script and make sure the LDAP entries are correct. Once that all works, we add the next group of commands and test that. We make sure the LDAP entries are still correct, and then check that the internal web space exists. Then we add the next step and test the entire thing again.

Step 4: Test It All Together

Finally, we test the entire thing. If we have tested each step as we added it to the program, there is actually very little testing to be done.

Programmers generally dislike testing. They want things to work on the first try. By integrating testing into each step along the way, the testing doesn't seem too laborious and, as a result, there is a lot less of it to do at the end.

Simple Things Done Often

Here are some automation examples that are simple things we do a lot. Windows system administrators take heed—these examples are fairly Unix/Linux-centric, but the general principles apply to all operating systems.

Command Shortcuts

Most command-line systems have some kind of alias facility. This enables you to create new commands out of old ones. The syntax is different for every kind of command line. Unix has many different shell (command-line) languages, the most popular being *bash* and *csh*. They are different in many ways, but what you'll notice here (mostly) is that *bash* requires an equals sign. I'll give examples for both shells.

> The *bash* examples will work for any shell modeled after the original Bourne Shell by Steve Bourne (/bin/sh), such as the Korn Shell (/bin/ksh), and the Z Shell (/bin/zsh). Likewise, the *csh* examples will work for any shell with csh roots, including the Tenex C shell (/bin/tcsh).

Getting to the right directory

For example, I often need to change directory (cd) to a specific directory that has a very long path. This is a good example of where an alias is useful.

Bash:

```
alias book='cd ~tal/projects/books/time/chapters'
```

csh:

```
alias book 'cd ~tal/projects/books/time/chapters'
```

Now I can type **book** whenever I want to be in the right directory for working on my current book. If I start working on a new book, I update the alias. (I've been typing "book" for the last six or so years!)

This not only saves typing, it records the location so that you don't have to memorize it. One less thing that you have to remember is always a good idea.

To make an alias permanent, you have to add the above line to your *.profile*, *.bashrc* (bash), or *.cshrc* file (csh). These files are only read at login, so either log out and log back in, or source the files to read them in again:

Bash:

```
. ~/.profile
```

csh:

```
source ~/.cshrc
```

(Note: the bash command to source a file is the period, or dot.)

An alias can contain multiple commands. Separate them with semicolons. Here's an example where we need to change to a particular directory and set an environment variable based on whether we're using the A system or the B system:

Bash:

```
alias inva='cd ~tal/projects/inventory/groupa ; export INVSTYLE=A'
alias invb='cd ~tal/projects/inventory/groupb ; export INVSTYLE=B'
```

csh:

```
alias inva 'cd ~tal/projects/inventory/groupa ; setenv INVSTYLE A'
alias invb 'cd ~tal/projects/inventory/groupb ; setenv INVSTYLE B'
```

Instead of using a semicolon, use && to indicate "Do this next command only if the first one succeeded." This can be useful to protect against running a command while in the wrong directory. For example, you want to go to a particular directory and write a timestamp to a logfile. However, if the cd fails (the server is unavailable), you don't want to accidentally create a log-file in your current directory.

Bash:

```
alias rank='cd /home/rank/data && date >>.log'
```

csh:

```
alias rank 'cd /home/rank/data && date >>.log'
```

 Don't try to turn one OS into another. Aliases are great, but don't overdo it. I've often seen people developing dozens of aliases so that they can type DOS commands in Unix. I think this is a bad idea. You're never going to learn Unix that way, and the next time you are on someone else's machine and don't have access to those aliases, you'll be stuck.

Hostname Shortcuts

If there are particular hostnames you type over and over, you can save some time by creating aliases. For example, if you are often dealing with a machine called ramanujan.company.com, you can create an alias (a DNS CNAME record) called ram.company.com. That's a little less typing.

The problem with this technique is that it can become a maintenance nightmare. If people start to depend on both names, you're stuck maintaining both names. So how can you create an alias that only you know about that won't bother other people?

Typically, if there is a machine I access a lot, I'm accessing it almost exclusively via Secure SHell (SSH). SSH is a secure (encrypted) replacement for *telnet* and *rsh*. You can also use it to copy files (*scp*, a replacement for *rcp*), and many programs, such as *rsync*, use SSH. Unix SSH (OpenSSH and its brothers) lets you set up host aliases for all users on a Unix machine or aliases that are private for you.

To affect only your SSH sessions, add aliases to the *~/.ssh/config* file. To affect all users of the system, add aliases to either */etc/ssh_config* or */etc/ssh/ ssh_config*, depending on how your system was configured. In this example, I create an alias, es, so that I don't have to type www.everythingsysadmin.com all the time:

```
Host es
    HostName www.everythingsysadmin.com
```

Not only can I use ssh es where I used to type ssh www.everythingsysadmin.com, but the alias works for all SSH-related commands: *scp*, *sftp*, *rsync*, and so on. In fact, scripts and programs that I can't change will automatically pick up these settings. Some examples:

```
$ ssh es
$ scp file.txt es:/tmp/
$ rsync es:/home/project/alpha ~/project/alpha
```

I need to use ssh es so often that I actually created a shell alias to reduce my typing further:

Bash:

```
alias es='ssh es'
```

csh:

```
alias es 'ssh es'
```

The result is that I can now type es on the command line to log into the machine, or I can use es to refer to the machine when using *scp* or *rsync*. Same two letters either way. Cool, huh?

It is tempting to create two-letter aliases for every server in the world. However, you will soon find yourself spending more time remembering your coding system than using it. Personally, I limit myself to a few common machines that I access via SSH.

The ssh_config(5) manpage lists many other configuration options. For example, there is one machine that I occasionally access that requires a very specific combination of options on the command line. (It's a home-grown version of the SSH server that not only doesn't implement all the features but gets confused if you try to negotiate anything it doesn't understand.) The command I have to type to get it just right is:

```
$ ssh -x -o RSAAuthentication=yes -o PasswordAuthentication=yes -o
ChallengeResponseAuthentication=no -1 peter.example.net
```

I could have set up a shell alias, but instead I can modify the SSH configuration, and all systems that use SSH will do the right thing. If a script that I can't modify uses SSH to reach that machine, these settings will still be used.

The lines in my ~/.ssh/config file look like this:

```
Host peter.example.net
    ForwardX11 no
    RSAAuthentication yes
    PasswordAuthentication yes
    ChallengeResponseAuthentication no
    Compression no
    Protocol 1
```

SSH clients for Windows tend to have a GUI that will let you save profile settings to be used for a particular host or hosts.

The more you learn about SSH, the more you can do with it. There are many good books and online tutorials on the finer points of SSH, such as *SSH, The Secure Shell: The Definitive Guide* (O'Reilly). If there is one thing every system administrator should, but may not, know about SSH, it is how to set up public/private keys to securely eliminate the need to type passwords when SSHing from one specific machine to another.

A Makefile for Every Host

This section applies to Unix/Linux systems. Windows folks might want to skip it.

Unix/Linux systems often maintain critical information in plain text files that are edited by hand. Sometimes, after editing a file, you have to run a command to inform the system that the information has changed.

SSH to the Right Server in a Web Farm Every Time

Suppose you have three servers: *server1.example.com*, *server2.example.com*, and *server3.example.com*. You have many web sites divided among them, and remembering which site is on which server is getting to be a drag. Is *www.everythingsysadmin.com* on server 1 or 3? You think it's on 3, but someone may have moved it to 2 when you ran low on disk space. Why try to remember at all? No need to set up a configuration file, just SSH to the web site's hostname! For example, type **ssh www.everythingsysadmin.com** and soon you'll find yourself on the right machine. OK, that's pretty obvious, but you'd be surprised how often people forget that it works!

Note: When the web pages move from one server to another, SSH will display a big, scary warning about the encryption keys changed. SSH remembers information about a host, and when you connect to the same machine and the information doesn't match, it displays a warning to indicate that there may be a "man-in-the-middle" security attack going on. When you see this, you should verify that the server really did change and then update your "known_hosts" file (delete the now-obsolete line). You can think of this as a way to notice when the server move has happened. Obviously if the data moves from server to server often, this will become annoying, making the technique less useful.

For example, after editing */etc/aliases* (part of sendmail, Postfix, and various mail-transport-agent packages), you must run the *newaliases* command. That's pretty easy to remember, right?

After editing Postfix's *transports* file, should you run the *newtransports* command? No, that would be too obvious. You must run **postmap transports**. And there is the *m4* command to run after editing .m4 files, and so on and so on.

Who has time to remember which command is used after which file is edited? Details like that are what computers are for.

make to the rescue! You might think of *make* as a programming tool—the program you run when compiling software. In reality, it lets you set up any kind of relationship involving the need to run a command to update one file if another changes.

make is one of the most powerful system administration tools ever invented. I hear programmers find it useful, too!

make has more features than Liz Taylor has had husbands, so I'll give a short introduction. (If you read the first two chapters of most books on *make*, you'll know 99 percent of what you need to for most system administration tasks and 10 times more than what your coworkers know.)

A Brief Introduction to make

make reads a configuration file aptly named *Makefile*. In this file, you will find recipes. They instruct *make* how to do its work.

Each recipe looks like this:

```
whole: partA partB partC
    command that creates whole
```

The recipe begins with the file that is going to be created, then a colon, and then it lists the files needed to build the main file. In this example, the recipe is about whole and establishes a relationship between it and partA, partB, and partC. If partA, partB, or partC is ever updated, then we need to (re)run the command that generates whole.

A real-world example helps:

```
aliases.db: aliases
    newaliases
    @echo Done updating aliases
```

This code means that if *aliases* is changed, regenerate *aliases.db* using the command *newaliases*. Then the recipe outputs "Done updating aliases" to announce its success.

Notice that the second and third lines of the recipe are indented. They must be indented with a tab, not multiple spaces. Why? My theory is that the original creator of *make* wanted to punish me every time I use cut-and-paste on a system that turns tabs into spaces. However, I don't take it personally.

The update doesn't happen automatically. You have to run *make* to make it happen:

```
Server1# make aliases.db
newaliases
Done updating aliases
Server1#
```

That's it! *make* read its configuration file, figured out that *aliases* was newer than *aliases.db* by checking the timestamp of the files, and determined that running *newaliases* would bring *aliases.db* up-to-date. If we run it again:

```
Server1# make aliases.db
Server1#
```

There's no output. Why? Because now the timestamps on the files indicate that there is no work to be done: *aliases.db* is newer than *aliases*. *make* is lazy and will calculate the minimum amount of work required to do what you ask. It makes these decisions based on the timestamps of the files.

Here's another *Makefile* code sample:

```
file1.output: file1.input
    command1 <file.input >file.output

file2.output: file2.input
    command2 file2.input >$@
```

In the first example, the command to be run uses stdin and stdout (file redirection using < and >) to read *file.input* and write *file.output*. The second example is similar, but the command takes the input filename on the command line and redirects the output to...what? Oh, $@ means "The file that this recipe is creating," or, in this case, *file2.output*. Why isn't it something simple like $me or $this? Who knows! You don't have to use $@, it just makes you look smarter than your coworkers.

make with no command-line parameters runs the first recipe in *Makefile*. It is traditional to name the first recipe all and have it run all the recipes you would expect as the default. This way, running *make* makes all the important recipes. It might not be literally all the recipes, but it is all the recipes you want to make by default. It might look like this:

```
all: aliases.db access.db
```

make with no options then makes sure that *aliases.db* and *access.db* are up-to-date. Since there is no command as part of all, no file called *all* will be created. Thus, *make* always thinks that all is out-of-date ("Doesn't exist" equals "Is out of date"). You'll soon see why that is important.

Remember that *make* is lazy. If *access.db* is out-of-date but the other file isn't, it just runs the commands to bring *access.db* up-to-date. In fact, if bringing *access.db* up-to-date required something else, and that required something else, and so on, *make* would very intelligently do just the minimum work required.

In addition to all, I usually include a couple of other useful commands:

```
reload:
        postfix reload

stop:
        postfix stop

start:
        postfix start
```

Think about what that means. If I run make reload, *make* is going to notice that there is no file called *reload*, so it will run postfix reload thinking that the command will create a file called *reload*. Ah ha! I fooled them, didn't I? The command I listed tells postfix to reload its configuration. That command doesn't create a file called *reload* at all! Therefore, the next time I run make reload, *make* will run the command again. In other words, if you want something to always happen, make sure the recipe simply doesn't create the file that *make* is expecting to create.

With the above code in my *Makefile*, I can reload, stop, and start postfix by typing make reload, make stop, or make start, respectively. If there are other things that should be stopped (for example, an IMAP server, web-based email client, and so on), I can include commands to do those things in the recipes. I don't have to remember all the commands.

This is a good time for me to point out a little lie that I told earlier. I said that each recipe begins with the file that is going to be created, followed by a colon, and then it lists the files that make up the main file. *make* doesn't know whether those files really make up the file to be created. There's no way it could tell. Those items listed after the colon are really just dependencies that must be up-to-date.

Here's a simple *Makefile* from a system that runs Postfix and includes recipes for rebuilding the index for aliases and access. You'll notice that at the top are some constants (NEWALISES, PDIR, and so on) that are used throughout the file. Also, a backward slash (\) at the end of the line is used to continue long lines:

```
NEWALISES=/usr/sbin/newaliases
PDIR=/etc/postfix
POSTMAP=/usr/local/postfix/sbin/postmap

# The "commands"

all: $(PDIR)/aliases.pag $(PDIR)/aliases.dir \
        $(PDIR)/access.dir $(PDIR)/access.pag reload

reload:
        postfix reload

stop:
        postfix stop

start:
        postfix start

#
# When aliases changes, generate the .pag and .dir files
#
$(PDIR)/aliases.pag $(PDIR)/aliases.dir: $(PDIR)/aliases
        $(NEWALIASES)

#
# When access changes, generate the .pag and .dir files
#
$(PDIR)/access.dir $(PDIR)/access.pag: $(PDIR)/access
        $(POSTMAP) $(PDIR)/access
```

Now I can edit either aliases or access and type **make**. I don't have to remember that the commands to update the indexes are extremely different. And I don't have to remember to tell postfix to reload its configuration each time because the all recipe includes that. The reload at the end of all will trigger that recipe every time.

make can also be useful for keeping files on various servers up-to-date. For example, let's suppose the *aliases* file in our example needs to be the same on both of our email servers. We decide that we'll update the file on this server, and push it to server2. That recipe might look like this:

```
push.aliases.done: $(PDIR)/aliases
    scp $(PDIR)/aliases server2:$(PDIR)/aliases
    touch $@
```

We push the file to server2 using *scp*, then touch a file called *push.aliases. done*. Since this file is created after the successful copy of the file, we can build recipes so that the push is only done if it's absolutely needed. We can also force the file to be recopied by simply deleting the *push.aliases.done* file and typing **make**. Traditionally, there is a recipe called clean that deletes all the *.done* files and other machine-generated files.

There is nothing special about files that end with *.done*. It is simply customary to name-flag or timestamp files with *.done* at the end.

Here's a complete example. There are two files that need indexing if they change: *aliases* and *access*. If either of them has been reindexed, postfix is told to reload. They also are both pushed to server2 if they change. Finally, the command cd /etc && make is sent to server2 if and only if one or more of the files has been pushed to it.

By carefully constructing the recipes with proper dependencies, and touching *.done* files where required, *make* will do the absolute minimal amount of work to bring the system up-to-date:

```
#
# Makefile for server1
#

NEWALISES=/usr/sbin/newaliases
PDIR=/etc/postfix
POSTMAP=/usr/local/postfix/sbin/postmap

#
# High-level "commands"
#
all: aliases.done access.done reload_if_needed.done push

push: push.done
```

```
reload:
    postfix reload

stop:
    postfix stop

start:
    postfix start

reload_if_needed.done: aliases.done access.done
    postfix reload
    touch reload_if_needed.done

clean:
    rm -f \
        $(PDIR)/aliases.pag $(PDIR)/aliases.dir \
        $(PDIR)/access.dir $(PDIR)/access.pag \
        push.aliases.done push.access.done reload_if_needed.done

#
# Recipes for particular files that need indexing/regeneration
#

# When aliases changes, generate the .pag and .dir files

aliases.done: $(PDIR)/aliases.pag $(PDIR)/aliases.dir
    touch $@

$(PDIR)/aliases.pag $(PDIR)/aliases.dir: $(PDIR)/aliases
    $(NEWALIASES)

# When access changes, generate the .pag and .dir files

access.done: $(PDIR)/access.dir $(PDIR)/access.pag
    touch $@

$(PDIR)/access.dir $(PDIR)/access.pag: $(PDIR)/access
        $(POSTMAP) $(PDIR)/access


#
# pushes
#

push.done: push.aliases.done push.access.done
    ssh server2 "cd /etc && make"
    touch $@

push.aliases.done: aliases.done
    scp $(PDIR)/aliases server2:$(PDIR)/aliases
    touch $@

push.access.done: access.done
    scp $(PDIR)/access server2:$(PDIR)/access
    touch $@
```

This *Makefile* is a good starting point for you to use on your systems. It is rather sophisticated because we do things to make sure Postfix isn't reloaded unless absolutely necessary.

With a *Makefile* like this, you no longer have to remember a multitude of commands and which ones should be used for which updated files. You never have to worry about forgetting to type a command. Many complicated procedures are reduced to:

1. Edit the appropriate file.

2. Type **make**.

make can be the ultimate tool for bringing together many smaller automated processes. Once, I had to merge the processes and procedures for three large networks into one. Each network had a different way of managing its aliases, hosts, and other administrative files. As I learned the procedures for each network, I constructed a *Makefile* specific to that network's master server. The high-level recipe names were the same in all three networks, but the commands they ran to accomplish the work were specific to each network.

The strategy was to create a new master server that would eventually replace all the legacy servers. Initially, the new master's *Makefile* simply initiated a *make* on the three legacy masters via *rsh* (this was long before *ssh*). I then migrated recipes to the new master one at a time. For example, first I decided that the new master would be the single source for the *aliases* file. I merged the aliases files of the three legacy networks and put the result on the new master. Once it was tested there, I added recipes on the new master to push that merged file to the legacy masters as if it were their own. I continued this process for each file or database.

Since each change was small and specific, I could test it incrementally. After literally hundreds of small changes, all the servers were "singing from the same songbook." At that point, it was easy to eliminate the legacy masters and let the new master be the authoritative master for all clients.

 Any file that is automatically pushed to other servers should always have a comment at the top of the file warning other system administrators where the file came from and where to edit it.

Here's the warning I use:

```
# THIS FILE IS MAINTAINED ON: server1.example.com
# Edit it with this command: xed file.txt
# If you edit this file on any other machine,
# it will be overwritten.  BE CAREFUL!
```

Since the previous note mentioned *xed*, I should explain what it is. There are many programs called *xed*, but this one can be found on *http://www. nightcoder.com/code/xed*. This program calls whatever editor you usually use ($EDITOR can be set to vi, pico, emacs, and so on) after locking the file. It is a must for any site that has multiple system administrators working on the same machine. If you are using RCS to track changes to a file, it does all the "check in" and "check out" work for you. This gives you infinite undo and a logfile of who changed what. If you find that a system has been acting funny for the last month, just check the log to see who changed the file a month ago and, well, be nice—we all make mistakes.

Hard Things Done Once

When we find ourselves doing something very difficult, automating the task records what we've done. When we do it in the future, it will be easier. This is how we build up our little bag of tricks.

Encapsulating a Difficult Command

Sometimes it takes hours to work out exactly the right command required to do something. For example, there is a program that creates ISO images, the kind you burn onto CD-ROMs. Its manual page describes hundreds of options, but to make an image readable by Windows, Unix, and Mac systems, the command is simply:

```
$ mkisofs -D -l -J -r -L -f -P "Author Name" -V "disk label" -copyright
  copyright.txt -o disk.iso /directory/of/files
```

Sure, you can do it from a GUI, but where's the fun (or ability to script) in that?

This command also lets you do things not found in most GUIs, such as the ability to specify a copyright note, author name, and so on.

This is a good example of something to work into a *.BAT* file (DOS) or a Unix/Linux shell script.

Here's a shell script called *makeimage1* that uses this:

```
#!/bin/bash

mkisofs -D -l -J -r -L -f -P "Limoncelli" -V `date -u +%m%d` $*
```

The `date -u +%m%d` sets the volume name to the current date.

One of the things that held me back from writing good scripts was that I didn't know how to process command-line parameters. Here are instructions for copying all the command-line arguments into a script.

The $@ in the *makeimage1* script means "any items on the command line." So, if you typed:

```
$ makeimage1 cdrom/
```

then the $@ would be replaced by cdrom/.

Since $@ works for multiple arguments, you can also do:

```
$ makeimage1 cdrom/ dir1/ dir2/
```

Then the $@ would be replaced by all three components. In the case of *mkisofs*, this would merge all three directories into the CD-ROM image. You can refer to $1, $2, and so on, if you want to refer to specific items on the command line. In this example, $1 would refer to cdrom/, and $2 would refer to dir1/.

Another thing that prevented me from writing good scripts was not knowing how to process command-line flags like scriptname -q file1.txt. Thus, if a script I wanted to write was sophisticated enough to need command-line flags, I would use a different language or not write it at all. It turns out *bash* has a feature called getopt that does all the parsing for you, but the manual page for Bash isn't clear. It tells you how the getopt function works, but not how to use it. Finally, I found an example of how to use it and have been copying that example time and time again. It isn't important how it works; you don't even have to understand how it works or why it works to use it. You use it like this:

```
args=`getopt ab: -- "$@"`
if [ $? != 0 ]
then
        echo "Usage: command [-a] [-b file.txt] file1 file2 ..."
        exit -1
fi
set -- $args
for i
do
        case "$i"
        in
                -a)
                        FLAGA=1
                        shift
                        ;;
                -b)
                        ITEMB="$2" ; shift
                        shift
                        ;;
                --)
                        shift; break
                ;;
        esac
done
```

This would be a command that has flags -a and -b. –b is special because it must be followed by an argument such as -b file.txt. It you look at the first line, the getopt command is followed by the letters that can be flags. There is a colon after any letter that requires an additional argument. Later, we see a case statement for each possible argument, with code that either sets a flag or sets a flag and remembers the argument.

What is this $2 business? What's the deal with the --)? What does set – mean? And what about Naomi? Those are all things you can look up later. Just follow the template and it all works.

(OK, if you really want to learn why all of that works, I highly recommend reading the *Advanced Bash-Scripting Guide* at *http://www.tldp.org/LDP/abs/html*.)

Here's a larger example that adds a couple additional things. First of all, it uses a function "usage" to print out the help message. An interesting thing about this function is that the "echo" lasts multiple lines. Neat, eh? Bash doesn't mind. Second, it makes sure that there are at least MINITEMS items on the command line after the options are processed. Finally, it demonstrates how to process flags that override defaults.

Please steal this code whenever you are turning a simple script into one that takes options and parameters:

```
#!/bin/bash

MINITEMS=1

function usage
{
    echo "
Usage: $0 [-d] [-a author] [-c file.txt] [-h] dir1 [dir1 ...]

    -d          debug, don't actual run command
    -a author   name of the author
    -c copyright    override default copyright file
    -h          this help message
"
    exit 1
}

# Set our defaults:
DEBUG=false
DEBUGCMD=
AUTHOR=
COPYRIGHT=copyright.txt

# Process command-line arguments, possibly overriding defaults
```

```
args=`getopt da:c:h -- "$@"`
if [ $? != 0 ]
then
    usage
fi
set -- $args
for i
do
    case "$i"
    in
        -h)
            usage
            shift
            ;;

        -a)
            AUTHOR="$2"; shift
            shift
            ;;

        -c)
            COPYRIGHT="$2"; shift
            shift
            ;;

        -d)
            DEBUG=true
            shift
            ;;

        --)
            shift; break;;
        esac
done

if $DEBUG ; then
    echo DEBUG MODE ENABLED.
    DEBUGCMD=echo
fi

# Make sure we have the minimum number of items on the command line.

if $DEBUG ; then echo ITEM COUNT = $# ; fi

if [ $# -lt "$MINITEMS" ]; then
    usage
fi

# If the first option is special, capture it:
# THEITEM="$1" ; shift
# Clone that line for each item you want to gather.
# Make sure that you adjust the MINITEMS variable to suit your needs.
```

```
# If you want to do something with each remaining item, do it here:
#for i in $* ; do
#      echo Looky! Looky!  I got $i
#done

if [ ! -z "$COPYRIGHT" ];
then
    if $DEBUG ; then echo Setting copyright to: $COPYRIGHT ; fi
    CRFLAG="-copyright $COPYRIGHT"
fi

LABEL=`date -u +%Y%m%d`

$DEBUGCMD mkisofs -D -l -J -r -L -f -P "$AUTHOR" -V $LABEL $CRFLAG $*
```

Building Up a Long Command Line

The best way to learn the Unix/Linux way of stringing commands together into one big pipe is to look over the shoulder of someone as she does it. I'll try to do that here by walking you through the steps I used to create a small utility.

Think Unix (Que) is an excellent book for learning how to link Unix/Linux tools to make bigger commands.

The single most powerful technology introduced by Unix/Linux is the ability to connect commands together like linking garden hoses. If you have one program that takes input and changes everything to uppercase, and another program that sorts the lines of a file, you can chain them together. The result is a command that converts the lines to uppercase and outputs the lines in sorted order. All you have to do is put a pipe symbol (|) between each command. The output of one command is fed into the next command:

    $ cat *file* | toupper | sort

For those of you unfamiliar with Unix/Linux, cat is the command that outputs a file. *toupper* is a program I wrote that changes text to uppercase. *sort* is the program that sorts lines of text. They all fit together quite nicely.

Let's use this to write a more complicated utility. How about a program that will determine which machine on your local network is most likely to be infected with a worm? We'll do it in one very long pipeline.

Sound amazing? Well, what this program will really do is find the hosts most likely to be infected—i.e., generate a list of which hosts require further investigation. However, I assure you that this technique will amaze your coworkers.

It's no replacement for a good malware or virus scanner. However, I picked this example because it is a good demonstration of some rudimentary shell-programming techniques, and you'll learn something about networking, too. When we're done, you'll have a simple tool you can use on your own network to detect this particular problem. I've used this tool to convince management to purchase a real virus scanner.

What's one sign that a machine is infected with some kind of worm? How about a quick test to see which machines are ARPing the most?

Spyware/worms/virii often try to connect to randomly selected machines on your network. When a machine tries to talk to a local IP address for the first time, it sends an ARP packet to find out its Ethernet (MAC) address. On the other hand, normal (uninfected) machines generally talk to a few machines only: the servers they use and their local router. Detecting a machine that is sending considerably more ARP packets than other machines on the network is often a sign that the machine is infected.

Let's build a simple shell pipeline to collect the next 100 ARP packets seen on your network and determine which hosts generated more ARP packets than their peers. It's sort of a "most likely to ARP" award. The last time I did this on a 50-host network, I found 2 machines infested with worms.

These commands should work on any Unix/Linux or Unix-like system. You will need the *tcpdump* command and root access. The command **which tcpdump** tells you if you have *tcpdump* installed. Sniffing packets from your network has privacy concerns. Only do this if you have permission.

Here's the final command that I came up with (sorry to spoil the surprise):

```
$ sudo tcpdump -l -n arp | grep 'arp who-has' | head -100 | \
awk '{ print $NF }' |sort | uniq -c | sort -n
```

The command is too long to fit on one line of this book, so I put a backslash at the end of the first part to continue it across two lines. You don't have to type the backlash, and you shouldn't press Enter in its place.

The output looks like this:

```
tcpdump: verbose output suppressed, use -v or -vv for full protocol decode
listening on en0, link-type EN10MB (Ethernet), capture size 96 bytes
    1 192.168.1.104
    2 192.168.1.231
    5 192.168.1.251
    7 192.168.1.11
    7 192.168.1.148
    7 192.168.1.230
    8 192.168.1.254
   11 192.168.1.56
```

```
  21 192.168.1.91
  30 192.168.1.111
101 packets captured
3079 packets received by filter
0 packets dropped by kernel
```

Ignore the headers. The middle lines show a count followed by an IP address. During my experiment, host 192.168.1.111 sent 30 ARP packets, while 192.168.104 only sent 1. Most machines rarely ARPed in that time period, but two hosts had four to six times as many ARPs as some of the other machines! Those were my two problem children. A quick scan with some anti-virus software and they were as good as new.

Here's how I built this command line. I started with this command:

```
$ sudo tcpdump -l -n arp
```

sudo means to run the next command as root. It will most likely ask for a password. If you don't use *sudo* in your environment, you might use something like it, or you can run this entire sequence as root. Just be careful. To err is human; to really screw up, be careless with root.

tcpdump listens to the local Ethernet. The -l flag is required if we're going to pipe the output to another program because, unlike other programs, *tcpdump* does something special with output buffering so that it runs faster. However, when piping the output, we need it to act more normal. The -n means don't do DNS lookups for each IP address we see. The arp means that we only want *tcpdump* to display ARP packets.

(If you are concerned about privacy of your network, I'd like to point out some good news. There isn't much private data available to your eyes if, at the sniffing end, you filter out everything besides ARP packets.)

Run the command yourself. In fact, you will learn more if you try each command as you read this. Nothing here deletes any data. Of course, it may be illegal to snoop packets on your network, so be warned. Only do this on a network where you have permission to snoop packets.

When I run the command, the output looks like:

```
$ sudo tcpdump -n -l arp
tcpdump: verbose output suppressed, use -v or -vv for full protocol decode
listening on en0, link-type EN10MB (Ethernet), capture size 96 bytes
19:10:48.212755 arp who-has 192.168.1.110 (85:70:48:a0:00:10) tell 192.168.
    1.10
19:10:48.743185 arp who-has 192.168.1.96 tell 192.168.1.92
19:10:48.743189 arp reply 192.168.1.2 is-at 00:0e:e7:7a:b2:24 19:10:48.
    743198 arp who-has 192.168.1.96 tell 192.168.1.111
^C
```

To get the output to stop, I press Ctrl-C. Otherwise, it will run forever.

If you get a permission error, you may not be running the command as *root*. *tcpdump* has to be run as *root*. You wouldn't want just anyone listening to your network, right?

After the header, we see these "arp who-has X tell Y" lines. Y is the host that asked the question. The question was, "Will the host at IP address X please respond so that I know your Ethernet (MAC) address?" The question is sent out as a broadcast, so we should see any ARP requests on our local LAN. However, we won't see many of the answers because they are sent as unicast packets, and we are on a switch. In this case, we see one reply because we're on the same hub as that machine (or maybe that is the machine running the command; I won't tell you which it is). That's OK because we only need to see one side of the question.

That's our data source. Now, let's transform the data into something we can use.

First, let's isolate just the lines of output that we want. In our case, we want the "arp who-has" lines:

```
$ sudo tcpdump -l -n arp | egrep 'arp who-has'
```

We can run that and see that it is doing what we expect. The only problem now is that this command runs forever, waiting for us to stop it by pressing Ctrl-C. We want enough lines to do something useful, and then we'll process it all. So, let's take the first 100 lines of data:

```
$ sudo tcpdump -l -n arp | head -100 | grep 'arp who-has'
```

Again, we run this and see that it comes out OK. Of course, I'm impatient and changed the 100 down to 10 when I was testing this. However, that gave me the confidence that it worked and that I could use 100 in the final command. You'll notice that there are a bunch of headers that are output, too. Those go to stderr (directly to the screen) and aren't going into the grep command.

So, now we have 100 lines of the kind of data we want. It's time to calculate the statistic we were looking for. That is, which hosts are generating the most ARP packets? Well, we're going to need to extract each host IP that generated an ARP and count it somehow. Let's start by extracting out the host IP address, which is always the sixth field of each line, so we can use this command to extract that field's data:

```
awk '{ print $6 }'
```

That little bit of *awk* is a great idiom for extracting a particular column of text from each line.

I should point out that I was too lazy to count which field had the data I wanted. It looked like it was about the fifth word, so I first tried it with **$5**. That didn't work. So I tried **$6**. Oh yeah, I need to remember that *awk* counts starting fields with 1, not 0. The benefit of testing the command line as we build it is that we find these mistakes early on. Imagine if I had written the entire command line and then tried to find this bug?

I'm lazy and I'm impatient. I didn't want to wait for all 100 ARPs to be collected. Therefore, I stored them once and kept reusing the results.

I stored them in a temporary file:

```
$ sudo tcpdump -l -n arp | head -100 >/tmp/x | grep 'arp who-has'
```

Then I ran my *awk* command against the temp file:

```
$ cat /tmp/x | awk '{ print $5 }'
tell
tell
tell
tell
...
```

Dang! It isn't the fifth. I'll try the sixth:

```
$ cat /tmp/x | awk '{ print $6 }'
192.168.1.110
192.168.1.10
192.168.1.92
...
```

Ah, that's better.

Anyway, I then realized I could be lazy in a different way. $NF means "the last field" and saves me from needing to count:

```
$ cat /tmp/x | awk '{ print $NF }'
192.168.1.110
192.168.1.10
192.168.1.92
...
```

Why isn't it $LF? That would be too easy. No, seriously, the NF means "number of fields." Thus, $NF means the field that is NFth fields in from the left. Whatever. Just remember that in *awk* you can type $NF when you want the last field on a line.

```
$ sudo tcpdump -l -n arp | head -100 | egrep 'arp who-has' | awk '{ print
$NF }'
```

So, now we get output that is a series of IP addresses. Test it and see.

(Really! Test it and see. I'll wait.)

Now, we want to count how many times each IP address appears in our list. There is an idiom that I use all the time for just this purpose:

```
sort | uniq -c
```

This sorts the data, then runs *uniq*, which usually eliminates duplicates from a sorted list (well, technically it removes any adjacent duplicate lines...sorting the list just assures us that the same ones are all adjacent). The -c flag counts how many repetitions were seen and prepends the number to each line. The output looks like this:

```
...
11 192.168.1.111
 7 192.168.1.230
30 192.168.1.254
 8 192.168.1.56
21 192.168.1.91
...
```

We're almost there! Now we have a count of how many times each host sent an ARP. The last thing we need to do is sort that list so we know who the most talkative hosts were. To do that, we sort the list numerically by adding | sort -n to the end:

```
$ sudo tcpdump -l -n arp | head -100 | egrep 'arp who-has' | awk '{ print
$NF }' |sort | uniq -c | sort -n
```

When we run that, we will see the sorted list. It will take a while to run on a network that isn't very busy. On a LAN with 50 computers, this took nearly an hour to run when not a lot of people were around. However, that was after the machine with the spyware was eliminated. Before that, it only took a few minutes to collect 100 ARP packets.

On your home LAN with only one or two machines, this command may take days to run. Hosts are required to cache the ARP info they gather, so after a machine is running for a while, it should be very rare that it outputs an ARP if the only machine it talks to (on the local LAN) is your router.

However, on a network with 100 or so hosts, this will find suspect machines very quickly.

We now have a very simple tool we can use during a worm attack. This doesn't replace a multi-thousand-dollar Intrusion Detection System or a good antivirus/antispyware/antiworm system, but it sure can help you pinpoint a problem when it is happening. Best of all, it's free, and you learned something about shell programming.

If you'd like to hone your shell programming skills, here are some mini projects you can try:

- *tcpdump* outputs some informational messages to stderr. Is there a way to stop it from outputting those messages? If not, how could we get cleaner-looking output?

- Turn this one-line command into a shell script. Put this in your *bin* directory so you can use it in the future.

- Take the shell script and expand it so that you can specify which NIC to sniff or other options you find useful.

- *tcpdump* can be programmed to only gather ARP "who-has" packets, so you can eliminate the *grep* command. Learn enough about *tcpdump* to do this.

- *tcpdump* has the ability to replace the functionality of head -100. Learn enough about *tcpdump* to do this. Is it the exact same thing as head -100? Is it better or worse?

- *awk* is a complete programming language. Eliminate the "grep" as well as the "head" arguments using *awk*. Why do you think I chose to do it in three processes instead of just letting *awk* do it all?

Using Microsoft Excel to Avoid Writing a GUI

Writing the GUI for an application can be 90 percent of the battle. Here's a lazy way to make the user interface: maintain the data in Microsoft Excel, but write a macro that uploads the data to a server for processing.

Once, I created an entire application this way. We had a web site that listed various special events. I was tired of updating the web page manually, but I knew the secretary wasn't technical enough to maintain the web site herself.

I started planning out a user interface that would let anyone do updates. It was grand—a big MySQL database with a PHP frontend that would let people log in, do updates, add new events, and so on. The system would then generate the web pages listing the events automatically. It was wonderful on paper, and I'm sure if I'd had 100 years to write the code, it would have been great.

Instead, I realized that only one person would actually be doing updates. Therefore, I gave her access to a spreadsheet that captured all the information that needed to be collected and to a macro that would save the file twice: once on the server as a tab-separated file and again as an XLS file. A process on the server would parse the tab-separated file and generate the web page automatically.

You can see the spreadsheet in Figure 13-2.

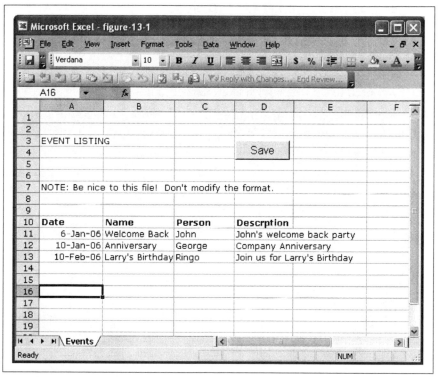

Figure 13-2. Event spreadsheet

Making the button takes a few steps.

First, use the macro recorder to do what you want:

1. Record the macro: Tools → Macro → Record New Macro.
2. Name the macro "Save."
3. Perform the actions to save the file as a tab-separated file on the network file server.
4. Save the file as an MS Excel Workbook (*.xls*) in your file area.

   It is important that the last place you save the file is the richest format (Workbook) because this choice sets the default save format. If someone saves the file using File → Save, you want it to default to this format.
5. Click Stop on the macro record toolbar.

Next, create a button and attach the macro to it:

1. View the Forms toolbar: View → Toolbars → Forms.
2. Click on the Button (looks like a plain rectangle).
3. Draw a button where you want it to appear in the spreadsheet.
4. When asked, select the macro created earlier.
5. If you need to edit the button later, Ctrl-click it.

Now, test this by clicking the button. Voilà! It works! Check the dates on the files to make sure that the file really got saved twice. (Yes, it may ask you twice whether it's OK to replace the file. Click Yes.)

If you want to clean up the macro a bit, that's easy, too. In fact, one of the first things I did was edit exactly where the file gets saved:

1. Go to the macro editor: Tools → Macro → Macros.
2. Select the macro we just created and click Edit.
3. Save and exit when you are done.

 In Microsoft macros, the line-continuation symbol is the underbar (_).

The final macro looks like this:

```
Sub Save( )
'
' Macro recorded 5/22/2005 by Thomas Limoncelli
'
    ActiveWorkbook.SaveAs Filename:= _
        "Y:\calendar\EventList.txt", FileFormat:= _
        xlText, CreateBackup:=False
    ActiveWorkbook.SaveAs Filename:= _
        "Y:\calendar\EventList.xls", FileFormat:= _
        xlNormal, Password:="", WriteResPassword:="", _
        ReadOnlyRecommended:=False _
        , CreateBackup:=False
End Sub
```

Now that I have the tab-separated version being stored on a file server, it was easy to create a script that could pick up that file, extract out the useful lines, and generate the web page from it.

I have since used this technique in many situations in which I didn't want to have to write a user interface and the user already had MS Excel.

Letting Others Do Privileged Operations

Often we are asked to create a way for normal users to do things typically permitted only by an administrative account such as *root*. This can be quite dangerous and should be done with great care.

In Unix/Linux, there is a program called *sudo* that lets system administrators give a person the ability to run a command as another user. It is very restrictive, requiring the system administrator to configure it to specify exactly which user(s) can run which command(s) as which other user.

For example, you can configure it to permit a particular person to run a command as *root*. You can rely on *sudo* to make sure that only the people you specify have the ability to run this command as *root*, but it is important that the program check the parameters to make sure that privileged users are able to overstep their bounds.

Any kind of system that lets "normal" people do "privileged" operations is a risky system to build. Computer security history is fraught with well-meaning programmers accidentally creating security holes that let people run any command as *root* or *administrator*.

If you aren't sure what you are doing, research security books and FAQs for advice.

For example, if it requires *root* to run the Unix *mount* command to access a CD-ROM. It is a bad idea to configure *sudo* so that the person can run the *mount* command as *root* with any parameters. He could crash the system or break security. It is much better if you configure *sudo* to let the person run a new command (say, *mountcd*) as *root*. This command will make sure that he has specified the particular CD-ROM drives that the user is permitted to mount (with a logical default), and mounts that drive. You also want to give him an (*unmountcd*) command.

I like to build three layers when I automate something for other people:

- **Layer 1.** A program that does the basic task.
- **Layer 2.** A program that the user will run, with *sudo*, that collects her input, validates it, makes sure she isn't trying to do anything fishy, and then calls the first program.
- **Layer 3.** A more user-friendly way to access these previous layers, such as a web interface or menu program.

For example, at one company, we had a process for pushing a new version of the company web site to the world. It involved three different web servers (actually they were virtual servers on two different machines, but those details aren't important).

www-draft.example.com
    The next release of our web site was developed here.

www-qa.example.com
    The draft site would be copied here for QA to check over. Once the copy was made, the files were immediately made read-only. If QA approved this site, we needed to be able to verify that these exact bits were copied to the live site.

www.example.com
    This was the live site that external people would see.

The web designers would ask the system administrators to copy their draft to *www-qa.example.com*. When the QA group approved the site, they would tell the system administrators to make the site go live.

Each of these two functions was automated:

readyforqa
    Copied the draft site to the QA site.

golive
    Copied the QA site to the live site.

Marketing demanded a way to make emergency updates when the QA department wasn't available. We created this command:

emergency-draft-to-live
    Copied the draft site directly to the live site after asking "Are you sure?" a few times.

These three scripts comprised Layer 2, which I mentioned earlier. Layer 1 was a script that did the actual copying of one site's data to another site, making a backup along the way, and setting files to read-only (changing the ownership of the files, too). Layer 1 had to be done as *root* because it was changing ownership of files and accessing machines via secured channels.

sudo was programmed as described in Table 13-1.

Table 13-1. Web update permission table

	Web developers	QA	Marketing
Readyforqa	X		X
Golive		X	
Emergency-draft-to-live			X

We actually went through the effort of having management sign off on this chart, with real signatures, to make sure they understood that they were agreeing to what they thought they were agreeing to. The political process to get this approved was the difficult part. It took weeks. Presenting the information to management in the chart form made it a lot easier for a decision to be made. They could understand and update the chart themselves until they were happy with it. Translating the final chart into a *sudo* configuration file was the easy part.

Per Layer 3, we decided to make an easier way for people to access these commands. We considered a web interface, but, in this case, the users were satisfied with a menu program that presented them with a list of options that ran the appropriate command.

The menu ran without any additional privileges (i.e., not under *sudo*), but called the Layer 2 programs using *sudo* as needed.

Summary

- Automation is great because it saves you time. It also permits you to push work to other, less-technical people.
- There are four types of problems that SAs typically deal with:
  - Simple things done once
  - Hard things done once
  - Simple things done often
  - Hard things done often
- "Hard things done once" and "Simple things done often" are the right things to try to automate. "Hard things done often," while tempting, is usually better served by off-the-shelf packages (commercial or free).
- To automate a process, first be sure you can do the steps manually. Then document each step, and make sure that you can automate each step. Then bring all of the steps together.
- You can save a lot of typing time by making aliases. This is true for command-line systems as well as for applications, such as SSH. Set the alias as close to the actual application as possible. For example, setting the alias in the SSH configuration file means all systems that leverage SSH will use the alias.
- The Unix/Linux *make* command is extremely powerful. It is not just for programmers. You can use it to automate system administration tasks. On Unix/Linux systems, especially servers, standardize on having a *Makefile* in /etc that automates common tasks such as reindexing aliases, cloning data, and so on.

- *Bash* and */bin/sh* shell languages are more sophisticated and powerful than you may realize. The examples in this chapter reveal how to parse command-line options and even how to write a small malware detector!

- When writing a long command line, test each part as you write it.

- When writing code for other people, the user interface becomes more important. There are tricks and techniques to creating useful user interfaces. You can avoid the issue by shifting all data entry to a program like MS Excel or by providing a menu system or web interface that lets people access higher-privileged systems.

- When writing code to let users do privileged operations, be extremely careful. Build on security tools that already exist and have good credibility, such as *sudo*. Use a permission table to explain to management who will have access to what. It is their job to manage risk and your job to help them understand the issues. Get approval before you deploy the system.

- As you move through your career, you will find yourself automating more and more tasks. It is a good idea to learn a programming language suited for system administration functions, such as Perl, Python, Ruby, or Shell, as well as operating-specific techniques like those featured in the O'Reilly *Cookbook* series mentioned previously in this book.

Epilogue

Congratulations. You've made it all the way to the end of the book. So now what?

First, I recommend you reread the book. We learn through repetition. If you reread (or skim) the book while the topics are fresh in your mind, it will have a strong impact.

Second, practice makes perfect. The more you practice the techniques in this book, the better you will get at them. Suddenly, you'll find yourself knowing the techniques so well that you'll be able to customize them and improve them in ways that make sense for your particular lifestyle or situation. One reader found that he was better able to manage his daily to do lists when he swapped the sides of his organizer where he put his schedule and to do items. Who knew? Whatever floats your boat! I just recommend you try my way first to get a sense of the system.

Third, accept slippage. Sometimes you will lapse into your old habits. That's OK, as long as you recognize it and get back to using the techniques as soon as you can. It might be helpful to reread the appropriate chapter for some inspiration.

Fourth, you might consider reading some traditional time management books, ones not written for system administrators in particular. This book focuses on the things specific to the system administration lifestyle and leaves a lot of general topics to the other books that cover them very well. I recommend *Getting Things Done* by David Allen (*http://www.davidco.com*).

What to Do with All Your "New" Free Time?

The techniques in this book may save you hours, if not days, each week. If you save a little more than an hour per day, you can get the same amount of work done in a four-day workweek.

So, what will you do with all this free time?

Please don't squander it. I beg you. When I first started applying time management techniques to my life, I used all the new free time I gained on my then-current addiction: reading more Usenet NetNews. I guess the contemporary equivalent is to spend it reading RSS feeds, blogs, web sites, and such. Many such things are time wasters. Please don't use your new-found free time to pack *more* time wasters into your life.

I have a better idea.

Use this new-found free time to fight injustice.

The most common injustice that I see every day is the way corporations steal our lives away from our families. We wake up one day to find that our children have grown up hardly knowing us, or that our significant others are leaving because they hardly see us. "How did the time pass so quickly?", we wonder to ourselves.

There used to be the so-called "implied social contract." We work for a company 40 hours a week and in return we are paid enough to live plus a pension to retire on. It was a fair deal. However corporations now expect more and more of our time with no increased benefit to us. Geeks typically work 60–70 hours a week only to be laid off en masse due to the bad business decisions of clueless CEOs that are paid hundreds, if not thousands, times our salary. When I was at AT&T/Lucent in the 1990s, we were constantly reminded that we should expect less job security from the company whether or not we did a good job. We were told to praise the shift from guaranteed pensions to "every man for himself" 401(k)s. And yet, in my final years working there, the management was shocked and dismayed to find less loyalty from the employees. Loyalty is a two-way street.

Want to do something radical? Revolutionary? Use the techniques in this book to reassert the 40-hour workweek and reclaim your family life:

- **Go home after you've worked 40 hours in a week.** Be as loyal to your employer as it is to you. Go home 8 hours after you've arrived each day or after working 40 hours a week.

- **Spend more time with your significant other(s).** Give him/her a kiss that lasts a full 12 seconds every day (not 12 little kisses; actually count to 12 for one long kiss. You'll be amazed at the difference!). Tell them how much you appreciate them. Schedule date nights. If your PDA has a "random" setting, schedule a random "I love you" call each day (and block out at least 15 minutes so it doesn't feel rushed).

- **Spend more time with your kids.** If you have children, spend time with them doing something other than watching TV. Not sure what to do? Try asking them. Still not sure? Go where geeks get all their answers: search Google for "free things to do with kids [your town name]". No kids of your own? Be the fun Aunt or Uncle you wish you'd had when you were a kid.

- **Call your parents and other important people in your life.** Schedule a periodic reminder to call your parents and block out a good hour for the conversation. They'll appreciate it, and you'll appreciate it even more when they're gone.

There are many other forms of injustice in this world. My parents raised me to believe that it was immoral to let people go hungry, that racism was bad because fairness means treating all people equally, and that peace was God's will. Therefore, my morals lead me to fight poverty, racism, and militarism wherever I can.

Find some injustice in the world that concerns you greatly and put your technical know-how into helping. Here are some ideas:

- **Help a non-profit that fights injustice, web edition.** Find their web site and offer to help maintain it. Better yet, install a Content Management System or blog software so that they can maintain it without your help. Make sure they have a one-click donation system like *http://www. JustGiving.com.*

- **Help a non-profit that fights injustice, PC edition.** Offer to visit their office once a week to check over their PCs and answer their general PC questions. Make sure they have virus/spyware scanners that update automatically. Make sure their data backups work. If they need new applications, help them find off-the-shelf solutions.

- **Join your school board.** As a geek, I was always dissatisfied with my school's lack of science education and the over-emphasis on sports. School board seats often go uncontested, or can be won with a campaign budget of a few hundred dollars. Then you have direct influence on the budget and priorities of your school system. Fund anti-bullying programs, chess clubs, straight-gay alliances, music, and the arts.

- **Run for public office.** The fact that there are so many ill-conceived laws governing technology is not going to change until enough geeks run for office.

Fighting injustice is like dropping acorns wherever you go. Sometimes, you return to a place and find something wonderful growing; other times, there is nothing. Most of the time, however, you'll never know how much you've changed the world or how many people's lives you've touched. You just have to trust that it was worth it.

Peace.

—Tom Limoncelli

Index

We'd like to hear your suggestions for improving our indexes. Send email to *index@oreilly.com*.

About the Author

Thomas A. Limoncelli is an internationally respected author and speaker on many topics, including system administration, networking, and security. A system administrator since 1988, he now speaks at conferences around the world on topics ranging from firewall security to time management. He has worked for Cibernet, Dean For America, Lumeta, Bell Labs/Lucent, AT&T, and Mentor Graphics. He and Christine Hogan co-authored *The Practice of System and Network Administration* (Addison Wesley). He holds a B.A. in Computer Science from Drew University in Madison, New Jersey. He publishes a blog on *www.EverythingSysadmin.com*.

Colophon

Our look is the result of reader comments, our own experimentation, and feedback from distribution channels. Distinctive covers complement our distinctive approach to technical topics, breathing personality and life into potentially dry subjects.

The animal on the cover of *Time Management for System Administrators* is a wolverine (*Gulo gulo*). Long admired for their strength, cunning, fearlessness, and voracity, wolverines are still a mysterious but respected animal. Native Americans considered them to be mythical trickster heroes and links to the spirit world. Wolverines have been personified and glorified in poetry and folklore for centuries:

> Picture a weasel—and most of us can do that, for we have met that little demon of destruction, that small atom of insensate courage, that symbol of slaughter, sleeplessness, and tireless, incredible activity—picture that scrap of demoniac fury, multiply that mite some fifty times, and you have the likeness of a Wolverine.

> —Ernest Thompson Seton, 1909

Wolverines are the largest terrestrial member of the family *Mustelidae*, which includes weasels, skunks, minks, and otters. Like humans and bears, wolverines have plantigrade posture—they walk on the soles of their feet—helping them to move easily through soft, deep snow. Wolverines thrive in very cold climates—they are found throughout the holarctic taiga and tundra in North America and Eurasia—and they do not hibernate. During the day and night, solitary wolverines alternate between sleeping and foraging for food. However, their habits are not entirely known because they are difficult to track and study due to their large home range and low population density.

The wolverine is one of the smallest and most powerful predators at the top of the food chain. In fact, if a wolverine were the size of a bear, it would be the strongest animal on earth. But wolverines are still ferocious despite their diminutive stature. They are solidly built and immensely strong—a wolverine can drag a carcass three times its size for great distances. Wolverines don't hesitate to attack sheep, deer, or small bears, but their diet mostly consists of scavenging rather than hunting. Wolves and cougars will retreat from a freshly killed carcass when a pack of wolverines challenges them. However, wolverines don't subsist entirely on large ungulates; they also eat squirrels, hares, and berries. When food is scarce, wolverines will return to an abandoned carcass and feed on the pelt and frozen bones; their powerful dentition and associated musculature facilitate this foraging.

For centuries, humans hunted wolverines for their luscious fur, which is valued because frost brushes right off of it. With dwindling numbers and a slow reproductive rate, wolverines are climbing up the endangered species list as nimbly as they climb trees.

Marlowe Shaeffer was the production editor and proofreader for *Time Management for System Administrators*. John Santini was the copyeditor. Colleen Gorman and Darren Kelly provided quality control. Johnna Dinse wrote the index. Loranah Dimant provided production assistance.

Karen Montgomery designed the cover of this book, based on a series design by Edie Freedman. The cover image is from *Wood's Illustrated Natural History*. Karen Montgomery produced the cover layout with Adobe InDesign CS using Adobe's ITC Garamond font.

David Futato designed the interior layout. This book was converted by Keith Fahlgren to FrameMaker 5.5.6 with a format conversion tool created by Erik Ray, Jason McIntosh, Neil Walls, and Mike Sierra that uses Perl and XML technologies. The text font is Linotype Birka; the heading font is Adobe Myriad Condensed; and the code font is LucasFont's TheSans Mono Condensed. The illustrations that appear in the book were produced by Robert Romano, Jessamyn Read, and Lesley Borash using Macromedia FreeHand MX and Adobe Photoshop CS. The tip and warning icons were drawn by Christopher Bing. This colophon was written by Marlowe Shaeffer.

CPSIA information can be obtained at www.ICGtesting.com
Printed in the USA
240739LV00020B/13/P

9 780596 007836